All the Books She Never Wrote

A Mother, A Son, & A Long Goodbye

Doug Bradley

Legacy Book Press LLC
Camanche, Iowa

Also by Doug Bradley

DEROS Vietnam: Dispatches from the Air-Conditioned Jungle

We Gotta Get Out of This Place: The Soundtrack of the Vietnam War (with Craig Werner)

Who'll Stop the Rain: Respect, Remembrance, and Reconciliation in Post-Vietnam America

The Tracks of My Years: A Music-Based Memoir

To my mom, Lucia Jean Basile Bradley,
for showing me the wonder of words.

"There is a mystery in all great writing and that mystery does not dissect out. It continues and is always valid."

—Ernest Hemingway

"There is an enduring tenderness in the love of a mother to a son that transcends all other affections of the heart."

—Washington Irving

Contents

chapter one

"Read Me a Story"

"Read me a story," my 99-year-old mother said, placing her withered hand on mine. We were in her cluttered bedroom in Madison's All Saints Catholic Retirement community which could exist anywhere in apostolic America. She was resting on her pillow with the tiny bluebell flowers. I was seated on the only usable chair in the bedroom, a stiff, hardbacked one that usually sat buried beneath fabric and yarn in a corner next to her dresser. Which was across from her makeshift desk that harbored her old Singer sewing machine. Her voice sounded a little like her sewing machine. I knew we were in unchartered territory because no one enjoyed reading books more than my mom. I gently stroked her wrist, asking it the questions I was hesitant to raise with the person whose body it belonged to. For the first time in her life, Lucy Basile Bradley was starting to look her age. It was unnerving to say the least.

"Sure, Mom, okay," I was sputtering a little. "What do you want me to read?"

"See that book on my nightstand," she tried to point, but was having a hard time lifting her head and getting her finger to go in the direction she wanted. "The one on top of the pile…I think it's called *Devil's Damnation*…Yes, that one."

"*Devil's Gambit*," I picked it up and stared at the cover, a painted tableau of menacing faces and circus clowns. "What's it about?"

Momentarily, she wasn't a frail, dying nonagenarian but a precocious schoolgirl trying to ace an exam. "There's this guy who at one time was a spy." Her weak voice lowered to a whisper as if one of the characters in the book would overhear our conversation. "Later, he was kidnapped by a bunch of Russians who brainwashed him. Or was it the Chinese? Any who, now he's got a magic act in a modern-day circus..."

"Sounds weird to me," I interrupted.

"No, it's really not that weird. His magician role is his cover, because he's actually back to being a spy, but there's this other really nasty guy who's on to him."

"What other guy? Is he in the circus too?"

"No, no." She seemed mildly annoyed, gently tapping my hand as if to communicate by Morse code. "The other guy, the bad one, is an honest-to-God villain. He kidnaps lots of people and tortures them, men and women he suspects might be spies or traitors."

"Jesus, mom, do you really want to be reading this crap?"

"It's not crap." She raised her voice about as high as it could go, which wasn't very high. It crackled a little too, as if there was something else trying to get out.

"I can't read very well anymore," she unhappily admitted. "I have trouble concentrating...I keep rereading the same lines." She paused. "It happens sometimes when I'm talking too." A longer pause, then a faraway look. "I keep wondering why I'm still here."

★★★

Why Lucy was still here was the exact same question we'd all been asking, privately and publicly. I sure as hell wasn't going to broach that inquiry with my dying mother whose current wish was to exit stage left as soon as possible. But talk about doing a 180. Ever since my dad passed away in 2009, my mom had been in high gear in the senior living fast lane, very feisty and extremely competitive. Up for just about anything and everything.

And then she turned 99. All of us—her family here, there, and everywhere—were thrilled that Lucy was on the on ramp to 100. What a celebration that would be. One hundred years of good living!

Not so fast. One bad fall on her April first birthday, followed by another in her kitchen a couple days later, landed my mom in the hospital for the requisite three-day Medicare stay before getting the boot to a nearby rehab facility. Lucy never acknowledged it, but I could tell she hated being in both those antiseptic spaces. Worse, she would miss our son Ian's Arizona wedding which she had been looking forward to ever since her grandson had met Mary Rowley. Ian and his grandmother had a special bond, you could say a friendship, one that extended to his fiancée Mary whom my mom decided the very first time they'd met that Ian indeed should marry Mary. And be quick about it.

As with many things, Lucy's instincts were spot on—the Ian-Mary nuptials were happening. And they had invited me to officiate at their wedding. But I was haunted by her absence, to the point where I blew a few of my lines and failed to bring the right amount of affection, humor, and charm to the festivities.

Undaunted, and a little broken-hearted, my mom kept her spirits up and worked like hell to "graduate" from the rehab facility as fast as she could, anxious to return to her tiny apartment and all those bad mystery novels she loved to read.

"Your mother is amazing," one of the underpaid night nurses said to me one evening when I was leaving the rehab facility. "I can't believe little Lucy is 99!"

Was there something about that number that bothered my mom? Its proximity to three digits, an entire century of living? She never said. Maybe the toll from all those years of taking care of somebody else—her elderly parents, then me, my older brother, and my dad, him for nearly 70 long years of marriage—and not tending to herself had caught up with her? Or did she miss her large, tight-knit Albanian-Italian family too much, anticipating, like all good Catholics, a reunion with her parents and ten siblings in heaven? I didn't know, and I was too hesitant to ask.

But Lucy's eventual return to her apartment at All Saints didn't do the trick. Quite the opposite. Almost immediately, she came down with an unrelenting, blood curdling cough that kept her awake all night. The coughing jags were amplified by debilitating vomiting. I was spending all my time by her side, annoyed and troubled by the coughing and puking, weary of cleaning up after her. Pissed at my Arizona brother Ron for not being there beside me, beside her. After tons of doctor's appointments and X-rays and blood tests and medications and hospice enrollment and hospice nurses and hired caregivers and more medications, Lucy, or "Lucia" as our friend Don liked to use her actual birthname, simply decided she'd had enough.

"I'm done," she informed me on Mother's Day, barely two weeks since she'd been back home. "I don't want to be 100. This isn't living." That afternoon was the last time her voice possessed any strength.

The off-white walls in her tiny apartment seemed to dim as she told me this. Her bed—the new one my wife Pam and I had just bought for her so she didn't have to use a stepstool to get into her old one—embraced all that was left of her. And the two old, brown, weathered nightstands, her wobbly desk with the heavy sewing machine, and her humongous dresser all heaved a sigh. Yet, her words weren't registering. She couldn't be telling me this…? But that determined look on her face was proof enough.

"Mom, what in the hell are you saying? Everything will be okay soon, and you'll get better." I gripped both her hands.

"No, it won't." She obviously knew something I didn't. "I've had a good life, and it's time."

I couldn't hold back my tears. "Mom, you c-c-c-can't…you can't do this. You can't just give up and…"

"And die?" she finished my sentence. "I don't want to be a burden on you and Pam. I'm ready to go."

I gave what was left of her inside that light blue night gown a big hug. *Jesus*, I thought, *my mother really wants to die?*

She rubbed my back and comforted me as I sobbed uncontrollably into her empty shoulder. Had we made her think she was a burden? What kind of son was I?

"You're a good son," she said as she kept rubbing, reading my mind like always. "But I don't want to live like this. Like I said, this isn't living. Who cares about 100?"

"Forget 100," I tried to challenge her, knowing how competitive she was. "You're as young as you want to be. The hospice nurses and the other caregivers—hell, all the staff at the rehab place—they all said you were like 79, not 99."

She smiled, an all too knowing smile. "They're not me. They don't know what I know. It's my time and I'm ready."

★★★

That conversation was almost three weeks ago, the same day my mom decided to stop eating. I couldn't argue with her then–hell all I did do was cry–and I wasn't going to argue with her now. Ron neither. He'd arrived from Arizona a few days before Lucy's declaration after I'd sobbed on the phone, admitting how overwhelmed I was by all this. Ron could always make little Lucy laugh and play cards, but even his old magic wasn't working. He'd spent the previous night and early morning with her and, as was our tag team routine, had gone back to our place to get some rest. Nice of my mother to drop the "I'm done" bomb on me. I looked back at my notes from that Mother's Day vigil to see if there were some clues, like the ones she'd always search for in her mysteries.

- Slept until noon
- Hospice nurse Megan arrives 12:30 p.m. Checks her vitals. Mom complains of chest pain and fatigue. Nothing determined…not sure what's going on? Lucy not happy with that news. "You must be missing something," she chides Megan. "Listen again!"
- Has a Lipton cup of soup at 1 p.m.
- Sleeps from 1:30 to 4:00. She cries out a couple times; once it sounds like she was saying "Dennis the Menace?"

- 4-5 Club crackers and cranberry juice at 4:20; throws up crackers and juice ten minutes later!
- Tells me she wants to die. Consoles <u>me</u>!
- Ron relieves me at 6:45 p.m. Doesn't think she's serious about wanting to die. Gives her Tylenol and Omeprazole. Back to sleep around 8 pm.
- Wakes up to pee at midnight. "No more food or drink," she tells Ron. "I'm done. They're waiting for me." *Who's they*? She doesn't explain…

No eureka moments there as far as I can tell. What am I missing? Not much has changed in the past three weeks except she sleeps a lot more and her skin tone has gone from off white to gritty gray, her eyes recessing into her skull. All of Ron's family came to say their last goodbyes, as did Ian and Mary. Our daughter Summer and husband Brandon are helping us manage, lifting everyone's spirits, especially Lucy's, when they bring their two little ones, Tess, three, and Bo, one, to see their great grandma.

"Why am I still here?" she habitually asks when she wakes up. "I figured I'd be gone by now," she said, a look of little girl disappointment on her face.

"I guess it's not your time," I remind her. *How was I supposed to know*?

"It's not fair. I should be gone by now." She still had that old paisana spunk and was not pleased with what was, or wasn't, going on.

"Mom, you can't just make this happen…" I stopped, realizing I'd made the mistake of seeming to talk her out of it.

"Why not? It's my time and I'm ready. There's no reason for me to still be here."

"But you *are* here, and so am I, so let's make the most of it." This usually meant our playing a couple games of two-handed pinochle or, in the evening, watching one of the British mysteries she loved on public broadcasting. Ron and I had moved her TV into her bedroom before he returned to Arizona.

"You know what I want." She was back to being in charge.

"And that is?"

"I want you to read me a story."

chapter two
Devil's Gambit

"How far did you get Mom?" I asked, lifting her most recent mystery off the nightstand which seemed near ready to collapse under the weight of boxes of Kleenex, medicines, ointments, a bell, a lamp, adult diapers, and a box of disposable gloves for her caregivers.

No response. Was she still breathing? For a moment, like so many of the moments in the days since she announced she was ready to die, my spirited mother looked like she'd given up the ghost, had gone to meet her maker, had cashed it in, bought her lunch, kicked the bucket, or whatever other metaphors there were to use. And then her eyes, deeper and deeper inside her head, would open and she'd pat my hand.

She was back. From where I wasn't quite sure.

"My bookmark's in there, isn't it?" A lifelong cat lover, Lucy's bookmark had a picture of a Siamese cat on heavy paper that sat above two silver metal clips that hooked to the top of each side of a page. I'd never seen a bookmark like this and figured no one else had one that was identical.

"Chapter 7," I proclaimed with a bit of dramatic flair. She perked up. I glanced over at her. "This isn't one of the chapters about torture, is it?" I asked warily.

"Don't be such a baby," she chided me. "Read."

"Giles Turner awoke with a start and took a quick scan of the room. A sink, a toilet, a bed. No rugs, no window, four walls and a large metal door, and one lone lamp hanging from the ceiling.

Giles then realized his hands were tied behind his back and his feet chained to the floor. And that head pain? How had that happened? He tried hard to remember, but he had no idea where he was and how he ever got there.

"Good morning Mr. Turner," came an automated sounding voice. "Or is it evening? Do you have any idea which it is? No matter. Time as you know it doesn't exist here. Every moment is the same as the last. And your last will come when you least expect it..."

Giles Turner was half listening and half figuring out where he was and how he could get himself out of there. The ropes on his hand would be easy, but the leg chains, that'd be a taller order. And then that large, reinforced steel door...

"Of course, if you give us the information we want," the voice continued," you could be out of here in no time, pardon the pun." A slight mechanical laugh.

Yes, that laugh, Giles recognized it. Anatoly Fedorov. Had to be. But how had he gained the upper hand? And speaking of hands, wasn't Fedorov minus one, thanks to him?"

I stopped, hoping my mother had dozed off.

"Why did you stop? It was just getting good."

"Mom, are you kidding? This is terrible. A long way from all those good Agatha Christie, Dorothy Sayers, and P. D. James mysteries you used to read."

"It's not that bad," she feebly protested. "Besides, I've read all the others. Twice for some of them…and this was the only mystery in the latest bunch of books the mobile library folks dropped off when I could still go upstairs and see what they'd brought." She sounded genuinely disappointed.

"I'm sorry Mom. Do you want me to go upstairs to see if there's a better mystery for you? One you haven't read lately?" I could tell from the look on her face that this wasn't a welcome suggestion. The last thing she wanted was to have to make another decision, especially after she'd already made the decision, the one to die.

"Mom, I'll make you a deal," I quickly shifted gears, trying to appeal to her established competitive side. "How about I read some of that mystery novel that you and I worked on together a couple summers ago?"

Silence.

"Mom, did you hear me? How about I read parts of *Saints & Sinners*, that mystery you and I worked on?"

"We didn't finish it," came her less than enthusiastic reply. "And as I recall, you were unhappy because you were doing all the writing and I wasn't. You said I wasn't pulling my weight."

Jesus, she never forgets anything. Several years ago, after my dad died, I assumed she needed a pick-me-up, so I suggested we collaborate on writing a mystery. There wasn't a plot or a motive or a detective or a whodunit she hadn't read, so why not put her vast knowledge to good use? *Wouldn't that be fun*? I naively thought. A welcome distraction from the loss of her bosom companion of 68 years. I suggested we use the All Saints Retirement Center, her own retirement community, as the setting and include some of the staff as characters. I explained that's where she could be the most help, not to mention her providing all the necessary mystery elements and plot twists.

But right away my mom argued that she needed a computer to be able to write her sections of the mystery, and when I balked at that, she pretty much stopped giving me her expert input. We'd had a similar argument about the cell phone she said she just had to have, the one that now sat unused, out of power, on her coffee table. And she was still having to pay the cell phone provider for the service she never used!

"Yes, but we got a good start." I was trying to turn this around. "Maybe if we read it aloud, we'll get some sense of how to keep it going. Couldn't be any worse than *Devil's Gambit*." I forced a smile.

"'Didn't uphold my end of the bargain,' I think is what you said." Again, she sounded like one of the characters in her mysteries, or else a femme fatale from a film noir.

"I wasn't upset. Honest. I just wanted it to have more of *you* in it than me. You live here, you know the dynamics of the place. And you've read all of this…this…mystery…stuff, and I haven't."

"You were going to say 'junk' again, weren't you?'

"What are you talking about?

"Just now, when you said 'stuff' you were going to say 'junk.' You always looked down on my reading mysteries."

"Mom, what's wrong? What's all this about."

"You know I'm right," she added and sat back.

This was a losing battle. We'd gone over this ground many, many times. I did want her to read more of the classics but only because I thought she might like them – *Gatsby*, *A Farewell to Arms*…Joyce, Conrad…Hell, even *Huckleberry Finn*. I tried this last summer with *Eligible* by Curtis Sittenfeld, a takeoff on *Pride and Prejudice* that's rooted in *The Bachelor* TV show I knew she liked to watch. But she didn't find *Eligible* all that funny. Too much sex too, she said.

What is my problem? I wondered. *If she only has a few…days? Weeks? Why not just humor her?* Back to *Devil's Gambit* I figured.

"I accept." She was patting my hand again.

"Accept what Mom?

"Your deal." She perked up. "I'll go with it?"

"With what exactly?"

"You can read *Saints and Sinners*. If we don't like it, or decide it's not worth working on, then…"

"*Devil's Gambit*?" I filled in.

"No, sweetie, you're not paying attention. *Saints and Sinners* and then… then… I'll have to come up with another writing assignment for you." She smiled mischievously.

"For us," I countered.

"No, I'm afraid not. Your old mom's writing days are over."

"But when exactly were your writing days?" I said that before I should have. Shit. Tears welled in her eyes.

"It was a long time ago," she spoke more to the empty bedroom than to me.

It was almost time for the hospice nurse to arrive and clean her up, change her bed, make her feel better. Something I wasn't doing very well.

"Mom, I'm sorry. I didn't mean to hurt your feelings. I didn't mean to complain about your not contributing to our mystery." I was sputtering but she'd struck a chord, her words tugging hard at my heart. "I'm sorry I never bought you a computer…I'm sorry we didn't let you move in with us after Dad died…I'm sorry…"

"Do this for me will you please?" She obviously wasn't listening.

"Do what Mom?"

"Bring *Saints and Sinners* tomorrow. We'll go from there."

"If that's what you want, Mom."

"You're a good son." She patted my arm. Then quickly added, "I'm 100 percent certain that Giles Turner knows Fedorov is his kidnapper and is responsible for those other killings." She pointed at the book that was still sitting in my lap. "It's really not that bad."

"Bye, Mom."

"Good night, sweetie. See you tomorrow…if I'm still here."

chapter three

"If you Say So"

Brandy, one of the overnight caregivers my wife Pam and I had recently added to the team of Lucy's caregivers, jumped to her feet when I opened the door to my mom's apartment. Morning had broken, and the light was coming in through the big sliding glass French door to my mom's little balcony, casting Brandy in a pale yellow back light, making her appear even larger than she was. Her voice was as quiet and sweet as her physique was large and commanding. She was cuddling her pillow and sleeping bag in her arms as she walked toward me.

"How was she?" I asked in a whisper, knowing the answer would be the same as the morning before and the morning before that.

"Perfect. No problems." Brandy always sounded so reassuring. "She rang the bell around 11 to get on the portable toilet and then again around 2 a.m. for some ice chips and pain medicine. She's been asleep ever since."

No sooner did Brandy finish telling me this and begin to leave than I heard my mom's little bell ringing every so faintly behind her closed bedroom door. Did she always know when I'd arrive? No break for me, again.

Brandy sensed my disappointment.

"I can go in if you like."

"No, that's okay," I said. "It's 6:45 and that's our deal. Will I see you tonight again?"

"Sorry, I'm off for the weekend," she corrected me. "Liz will be here all this weekend. She gave everyone off for the Memorial Day Weekend."

Liz was our "death doula" as she called herself, although that title was way too off-putting for me, so I referred to her as my mom's medicine woman. Liz was kind and patient—centered, smart, and oh so reassuring. Among her many caregiving experiences, auburn-haired Liz with the billowy, colorful dresses had once been a nurse with hospice. Which had something to do with her training to become a death doula.

"Nothing against hospice," she began during one of our first meetings, "but they don't get death right. They make the folks in their care fearful of dying when it's just another part of living. In a way, death is a beautiful thing."

If you say so, I thought, way more concerned with the dynamic between my mother and Liz than any death with dignity mumbo jumbo. But she was bright and cheery, starting her own business, and had assembled a cadre of competent caregivers who could fill in ably for me and hospice. More than fill in, really, because now several weeks into this, Pam and I were worn out, especially since Ron had returned to Arizona after his three-week vigil. Plus, hospice was spread so thin they didn't seem to have that much time for some old lady who'd decided she wanted to die and couldn't.

My mom liked Liz and most of her crew but, of course, preferred my company, and Pam's, when she was able to fill in for me. I didn't want to waste my time thinking about what all this was costing. Mothers aren't something you put on a debt ledger or liken to dollars and cents. Liz admitted that the overnight caregivers' time would be sizeable but that she'd help us out this weekend by being here herself. Maybe she would give us a reduced rate? "Stop that," I told myself. This is your mother!

The bell sound again. Brandy touched my wrist as I moved toward the door.

"You're doing a great job," she reassured me. "The times she's awake when I'm here, Lucy only talks about you. She sings your praises. You make her happy. You make her feel loved."

"Thanks," I mumbled, choking up a little. "It's just sometimes…" and I started to sob. Brandy started to lean toward to give me a re-assuring hug, but the bell sounded again, and I headed toward my mom's bedroom door.

"Thanks again, see you tonight." I waved at Brandy.

"Tuesday night," she reminded me as she exited.

"Good morning Mom," I smiled, leaned over, and kissed her forehead. "How was your night?"

"Who were you talking to?" she asked.

"Brandy. She just left."

"How much are you paying her?"

"Not that much. Why do you ask?"

"It's silly to pay someone to just sit around and sleep." She paused. "It's not like you have a lot of extra money to hand out."

I knew where this conversation was going to go—nowhere good for me, so I cut her off.

"Mom, Liz and her team are doing a great job. They all love you. It is not a burden. You're not a burden. So, let's not worry about any of that."

"If you say so." Little Lucy wasn't conceding anything

"So, what do you need?"

"What?" she seemed puzzled.

"You rang the bell, so what can I get you."

"YOU," she smiled. "I heard you come in…"

As much as she seemingly wanted to see me, after a few pats on the hand and some ice chips, my mom fell back asleep. I closed her door and entered her orderly little kitchen, even tidier thanks to Brandy who'd washed and put away all the dishes I'd left from yesterday. Started to clear out one of Lucy's over-stuffed cupboards too. I made a point to tell my mom that.

The dark, two-person cherrywood dining table was pushed up against the left wall as always. The even darker chairs stood at attention at either end. Undoubtedly the most uncomfortable chairs anyone has ever sat in. My mom tolerated them and would chide me when I complained whenever we had dinner together in her kitchen, or when we played cards, which is what she liked to do morning, noon, and night. Pinochle being her game. "A poor man's Bridge," she liked to say.

The old kitchen light with blue sailboats on the lampshade and the tiny pull-string chain rested above the table. Her fridge was a mosaic of family photos, my two children and Ron's four, her seven great grandchildren in various poses and settings from Arizona to Montana to Wisconsin. Doctor's appointment and notes, a list of her medicines, and lots of cat magnets with all kinds of positive messages about life and sunshine and having a "purr-fect day." And her favorite of all, a long cloth calendar that she'd get from us every Christmas. Pam and I had begun the cloth calendar tradition years and years ago, and now our grandkids (via us) were the providers. Their names in big, bold letters stood out at the bottom of the calendar. This year's theme was "Imagine the Pasta-bilities" and featured a very large, very fat Italian chef whose sizable white apron had the months of the year on it. He was holding a large pasta spoon in his left hand and, of course, had a huge, very Italian looking mustache. My mom said the chef looked a lot like her older brother Alphonse. I should say departed older brother. Of all 11 Basile offspring, six males and five females, Lucy was the only one still here.

As I did every day after I arrived, I took out my trusty red notebook and wrote down whatever notes the caregivers had left for me. It was always a short, uneventful report. So, I'd spend the rest of my sentry time brewing and drinking coffee, reviewing the other notes I had from hospice nurses and doctors and caregivers…and then write some maudlin poetry.

Or fall asleep, which I must've done this morning because the next thing I knew, my mom's bell was tinkling away in her bedroom.

"Where were you?" she asked pointedly when I re-entered her room.

"I must've fallen asleep," I admitted, rubbing my eyes.

"You're doing too much. You need to take a break. Pam too."

"Mom, I dozed off a little. I didn't pass out from exhaustion. I'm okay."

"If you say so."

Second time I'd heard that response today, so I knew that I'd pay for both of these concessions later. Little Lucy seemed to keep a running score in her head and would always circle back to whatever argument she thought she should've won. But in a nice way, she'd remind me.

"Can you get me some ice chips, please. And a couple Tylenol arthritis…And I need to get on the commode. Oh, and some new undies, too, these are a little damp."

I now had a full list of chores to complete. Maybe I would have to try to get Liz over here a lot more this weekend? My mom was still talking, likely dispensing more orders.

"Liz said she could get a cat to come pay me a visit."

"Liz said what?" I was beyond puzzled.

"She says that there are pet services that will bring animals to visit people, make them feel better," my mom explained.

"And?" I sensed something else coming.

"And she says you might need to be here because of scheduling."

"Mom, you need to give me more of a heads up."

"I just did, didn't I?" She looked crestfallen.

Time for me to pivot. "So, when is your feline friend paying you a visit?" I forced a smile.

"That's just it, Liz doesn't know. That's why she needs you on back up. Turns out there are plenty of dogs available for visits, but only two cats and one of them is sick."

Is this some new circle of hell? I wondered. Dante had nothing on my mom, who apparently now needs me to do some kind of cat health intervention.

"So, do we just wait or what?"

"Ask Liz," Lucy shot back. "But make sure she doesn't charge you anything extra."

Time for me to stop asking questions and go home and get some rest. It was going to be a long "holiday" weekend…

chapter four

"Oh when the Saints..."

Liz looked exhausted when I relieved her Sunday morning, so I decided to suck it up and give her a rest, volunteering to take over the rest of the day and the Sunday overnight. That way maybe she could come back fresh on Memorial Day.

"You're a sweetheart," she thanked me.

Of course, I totally forgot to ask her about the cat visitation.

I brought a stack of papers with me, deciding the time would go faster if Mom and I got moving on *Saints and Sinners*. But when she signaled with her bell around 10:30, she looked annoyed at what I was holding.

"Hi Mom. How are you feeling?"

"I'm still here." She gave her usual dejected reply.

"Chin up," I smiled. "It's a beautiful day, and you'll have me all day and all night."

"Wonderful."

"And I brought along our story to work on."

"Is that what those papers are?" her voice perked up. "I was afraid those were bills from Liz. She and her people really don't need to be here so much."

"Mom, I'd love to take care of you all the time but I can't. Liz is a nurse and she knows what she's doing."

"What about the hospice staff?" She probed in her Perry Mason way. We'd gone over this territory multiple times but she was not going to let it rest. During one of my many May meltdowns, Pam and I decided we had to get extra help, especially overnight. Sure, Liz and her team cost money, but every time either one of us slept over at my mom's apartment—and it was usually me—we either couldn't sleep or we itched like crazy. Or both. Those damn cats she and my dad had in their previous apartments for so many years, none of which I liked, must've put a curse on me and left cat hair behind because I'd itch and scratch all night and then go back home tired and sneezing! And now she wants another one to come and pay her a visit!

"Mom, the hospice nurses are only able to be here during the week for a couple hours each day. Liz and her staff pick up the slack."

"I'm slack am I?"

"Not what I'm saying."

She grew quiet.

"You want to die, mom, remember? You're not eating. Pretty soon your body will begin to shut down. You need competent professionals here to take care of you."

"Well, when you put it like that," she moaned. I couldn't tell if she was still perturbed, distraught, or what. Then she got a look on her face that told me she'd filed this disagreement away in her Lucy vs. Douglas vault. I'd hear about it again someday, because she never let things go and she hated to lose an argument. Or a game of any kind.

"Let's see what you've got there." She changed the subject.

"Do you remember where we left off?" I asked.

"Start at the beginning please."

"Okay. Here goes." I grabbed my stack of papers and started to read.

"Father Seamus Paul navigated his Ford F-150 through the driving rain and swirling winds."

"What's a Ford 150?" she asked.

"It's an older model pick-up truck."

"Why would a priest drive a pick-up truck?"

"It tells the reader a little about him, show that he's different, not your usual priest." I was sounding a little defensive.

"I've never known a priest who drove a pickup truck," she wasn't budging.

"Okay, I'll change it." I was done arguing.

"Father Seamus Paul drove his car through the ..."

"What kind of car?"

"Any kind of car. Pick a car."

"Maybe a Ford Falcon? We had two of those once."

"Yes, we did, Mom, but they don't make them anymore."

"What about the car you drive? What's it called? An accurate?

"Acura."

"Make it an Acura then."

"Father Seamus Paul drove his Acura through the ..."

"Why did you name him Seamus?"

Impulsively, I threw down the several pieces of paper I'd brought along with me. I didn't have the patience for this. My mom looked puzzled, making me regret what I'd just done. The poor woman is dying, and I lose my temper? "Get your head out of your ass," I scolded myself.

"Is something wrong sweetie?" She asked me so innocently and sweetly that all I could do was smile.

"No, Mom, nothing's wrong." I patted her hand. Did either of us really need this now? I was too defensive about my writing and my mother, well, she was my mother so there was always a hint of disapproval in her response which was, of course, the last kind of disapproval I wanted to hear.

"Keep the pickup."

"What?"

"Keep the pickup truck," she repeated, "in the opening. Now I'm curious about what kind of priest would drive a pickup truck. That's good."

"Whatever you say Mom." I picked up the papers I'd tossed on the floor. "And the name *Seamus* indicates he's Irish," I added. "Plus, it's a play on *shamus*, which is another word for detective."

Lucy was smiling broadly.

"What is it Mom?"

"That's really good." She paused. "And here I thought you weren't paying any attention to the mysteries I was reading and telling you about." Another pause. "You have so many clever things going on in the very first sentence."

"Thanks, Mom," I was almost blushing. Over the years I got a lot of love from my mom but not an overabundance of compliments. She would usually compliment me to others.

"Now, let's see what kind of mischief Father Paul can get into," she motioned for me to read on.

"Father Seamus Paul navigated his Ford F-150 through the driving rain and swirling winds. "It was a dark and stormy night," he recited out loud and smiled, recalling how much he liked it when Snoopy, his favorite Peanuts' character, would quote that famous line from the old Bulwer-Lytton novel.

But this was no time for smiling. The phone call Father Paul had received not only interrupted his sleep, but it had left him scratching his head. Good thing his trusty Ford pickup could practically drive itself to the Old Saints Retirement Center.

"Father Paul? Father Seamus Paul?" the unfamiliar, mechanical-sounding voice asked.

"Yes," he replied. "This is Father Seamus Paul."

"Father, you're needed right away at Old Saints. One of your flock is in need of shepherding."

"Who is this?" Father Paul raised his voice.

"An angel of mercy," the voice replied. "Apartment 159, Old Saints. Be sure to bring your extreme unction."

The rain kept falling and the priest's pickup kept moving, but Father Paul was lost in thought. Who even knew, or used, the term "extreme unction" these days? And who said things like "flock" and "angel of mercy"?

And why did that voice sound so, so, un-human and ominous?

The driveway to Old Saints approached as Father Paul's Ford took its usual left and right turns into the parking lot. At this late hour only one light shone in the west wing of the retirement complex. Probably apartment 159, the sleepy priest surmised.

Father Paul stopped the car, turned off the motor, and pulled up the hood on his windbreaker. He reached behind his seat to grab a black bag filled with his priestly accoutrements and got out of the truck, just in time to hear what sounded like a cry or a scream, coming from inside the building. He started to jog toward the complex, only to look back to see his old Ford sliding backwards down the driveway toward a row of cars near the small hill overlooking the patios of several Old Saints apartments.

"Jesus, Mary, and Joseph," the anxious priest shouted, wondering how he'd forgot to put the truck in gear and set the parking brake. He thought he could still hear a noise inside the complex, but his immediate focus was rescuing his vehicle.

As Father Paul turned back around, the wind swirled, nearly lifting the hood of his parka off his head. Then all sound faded away, and everything went black."

★★★

"Uh, oh," my mom sounded concerned.

"What is it, Mom?"

"Father Paul is in a pickle." She gave a wry smile, relishing the reference.

I smiled back. "Right after this sentence, I put a line in there with three asterisks to indicate a scene break," I explained. "It's a visual clue that the scene has changed."

No response.

"Mom, did you hear me?

"Yes, I heard you." Her eyes were closed. She looked like she was searching hard for some fact or thought or memory, reminiscent of her buddy Giles Turner in *Devil's Gambit*.

"They do that all the time in my mysteries," she perked up, relatively speaking. "I'm guessing Father Paul wakes up after a while in the next scene. Keep going."

If you have all the answers, why didn't you write this yourself?
I wondered.

"Well if it isn't our old friend Father Flatfoot," the voice sounded familiar enough but Father Paul was having a tough time making out a face.

"You should stick to saving souls and let us round up the sinners." There was a slight smile on the brown face looking down at him, one that the priest now recognized as belonging to Melvin Williams, Madison chief of police. Father Paul and Williams had been cadets together way back when, and Williams was his deputy when Seamus Paul abruptly bolted from the police force to the priesthood. That story occupied the local newspapers for days on end, and even now, years later, whenever there was a story about a cold case or some reference to Father Paul's ecclesiastical work, a reporter would always make some snide reference to his solving crimes vs. saving souls, often less politely.

"Hold on a minute."

Here we go again. "What is it, Mom?"

"How did you come up with this angle, the priest being a former cop?"

"Does it matter?"

"Yes and no," I could see the wheels turning, lots slower now since she was dwindling daily without any food intake.

"What's the yes and what's the no?"

"Maybe it's yes and yes." Her logic was beyond me at this point.

"Can I keep going?"

She kept silent. More wheels. "I think it works," she announced. "Writers are always giving their characters a whatchamacallit, a behind the back story?"

"Back story," I corrected her.

"Yes, that's it," she smiled. "And I like what you're doing with Father Paul's black story."

She paused, not realizing she'd gotten the phrase wrong again. There was a lot she wasn't realizing anymore. And yet every time I thought that was the case and prepared myself for the last goodbye, my mom would surprise me by relating the details of a conversation I'd had with Liz or one of the hospice nurses. Or something I did when I was a little kid. Life, her life, had become this thread of disparate memories, conversations, experiences, and people. It reminded me of her knitting, which she was so good at and did most of her life. Stitch after stitch, row after row, breath after breath. I think it helped center her. And now it's helping her to go up and down those rows, all the rows she ever knitted, and pick out a stitch here—story about Dad—or a stitch there—something Liz said to me—and keep them there alongside all the other rows, every stitch.

"What's the holdup?" Dying Lucy sounded impatient.

"Sorry, Mom. Where were we?"

"The police chief is helping Father Paul."

Stitch. Row. Maybe all those 99 years were right here for the remembering?

"Good to see you, Melvin," Father Paul muttered. "Dare I ask what happened and where I am?"

Williams smiled. "You're in the lobby of Old Saints, padre, and your Ford pickup is adorning the hood of somebody's Honda Accord. I thought you God squad types knew how to drive."

Father Paul was being pulled to his feet, his head still trying hard to make sense of any of this. He didn't appreciate the fact that his old sidekick was making jokes at his expense.

"To top it off, it looks like you ran into the security locked front door and knocked yourself out!" Williams added. "That's worth at least three Hail Marys and a good Act of Contrition."

"Mustn't have set the parking brake," Father Paul offered, beginning to come around. He looked directly at Williams. "And what in the world are <u>you</u> doing here?"

"Was on my way home and heard the scanner say something about a Ford pickup running amok in the Old Saints parking lot, so I decided to check out what was going on. Made a wild guess and figured I'd find you here." Williams paused. "I had

a hunch it might be you out doing some of God's work late in the evening."

Williams steadied Father Paul on his feet. The priest suddenly remembered why he'd come to Old Saints in the first place.

"Melvin, I didn't fall or pass out, I was knocked out!" The priest showed the bump on his head to his old colleague. "And I was summoned here by a phone call that, well, that scared the you-know-what out of me."

"Old buddy, you've been watching too many crime shows on TV," Williams joked. "The only fatality around here is the little Honda that got attacked by your big bad pickup—and maybe your ego a little. Let's take a look at that bump."

Father Paul pulled away from the muscular detective. "Melvin, forget it I'm fine. And enough of your sarcasm. We have to find Peggy the resident manager and get into one of these apartments!"

I looked up. My mom had a huge smile on her face. Where was she now? Somewhere back with her six brothers and four sisters in that big old house of her sunny childhood? That's what she usually mentioned when she woke up. Or else cooking in her mother's kitchen, or gardening somewhere. I touched her hand ever so slightly.

"That was fun," she murmured faintly. "It's better than I remember from before." She looked as if she'd been on a long journey, or else had been hit on the head like Father Paul.

"Now, let me rest."

I placed my hand on hers, leaned over, and kissed her forehead. I had to lean down a little further because, like everything else, her forehead was retreating into her skull. I gathered my papers, closed her door, and sat in the kitchen, wondering, as I did every time I left her side, if I'd just said my final goodbye…

chapter five

Visiting Hours

More early mornings. More caretaker handoffs. Fewer undisturbed evenings. More, lots more, of Liz and her resourceful staff. Less of the spread-too-thin hospice folks. More money out the window…and a slew of visitors from the many nooks and crannies of All Saints. I only discovered this to be the case when I took an afternoon shift for one of Liz's caregivers…and in they came in droves. Sometimes not even knocking! Had they always been dropping by when I wasn't on duty?

"Lucy's a sweetheart," proclaimed a trio of elderly female admirers as they breezed past me into my mother's room to give her greetings and gossip.

"Your mom really gives me a hard time at pinochle and euchre," one of the few older men on the premises admitted sheepishly as he came to say hello. He introduced himself as Inky, which I hoped was a nickname. "She always elbows me in the ribs, or hits me on the arm, when I get the best of her. But more often than not, she wins."

Could those have been signs of affection from my mom? But as I scrutinized Inky—thin, scrawny, and ill at ease—I concluded he was not my mother's type. Whatever that was, her deceased husband notwithstanding.

"Oh, your mother's an All Saints celebrity," Sally, another of her silver-haired fans informed me as she poked her head in the door a few hours later. "Without her, we wouldn't have a weekly pinochle game. Or such fierce competition in the Wii bowling league. Everybody loves her, except when she wins. Which she does a lot."

Had my mom always been this competitive at games? And a ringleader to boot? That wasn't the impression I had growing up, but in the nine years since my dad died, she'd taken on a new life, one full of vigor, games, and socialization. Where had that been all those years? Stifled? Suffocated? Buried most likely since she was female and the youngest of 11 Basiles, forced to stay home and take care of elderly parents, denied the chance to continue her education, stuck with a needy guy like my dad for nearly seven decades. Lesser people, wimps like me, would have crumbled under the weight of all that obligation. But it just made my mom live her last years with added gusto.

As the word about Lucy's condition reached the ears of the greater All Saints neighborhood—Catholics being especially good at expanding their empires—I felt like a hall monitor those late mornings and occasional afternoons when I'd hold down the fort. I figured the timing of the visits must've coincided with the regular pinochle games or Wii bowling matchups. Without my mom there to preside, those activities probably weren't as lively, or competitive.

I did my best to keep it to two visitors at a time, but some days a line formed outside her apartment. Luckily, most folks didn't stay long. Not sure my ears could've handled it if they did. Just because my mom was dying didn't mean she was deaf—she always wore her hearing aids, but that didn't stop her many admirers from shouting.

"HOW ARE YOU FEELING?" came the usual first volley. In her weakened condition, my mom wasn't able to respond at a similar decibel level, so the same question would come again, followed by a chorus of "POOR DEAR" and "I'M SO SORRY"s. Every now and then my mom would remove her hearing aids, a survival mechanism I surmised.

Curiously, as I watched the stream of All Sainters come and go, most of them women in their late 70s and 80s, I noticed their slow, yet graceful movements, their quiet elegance, how their eyes shone with a bright something I couldn't describe. How they were always smiling. Happy, yes, but curious too…

And then it hit me. My mom's visitors would make the perfect characters for our mystery! All I had to do was ask her a few questions about each of them and, voilà, we'd have the entire cast we needed to get our story moving.

Or not?

I ushered out the last of the guests and bounded into my mom's room, brimming with my new idea for the story. But she was fast asleep, looking oh so worn out and exhausted from a long afternoon of smiling and nodding. I held her hand and made a solemn promise—adding a "cross my heart and hope to die" for good measure—that from now on nobody would be allowed in to see my mom without an appointment. And then only one visitor at a time!

A knock on the door. I exited the bedroom quickly, agitated that somebody from All Saints would be back already.

"Is Lucy available?" A tall, elderly priest peered beyond me into the apartment, his voice a loud whisper.

"Hello…Father. Lucy's sleeping right now. Can I help you?"

"I heard the news and wanted to stop by and give her comfort. Maybe hear her confession."

I almost laughed out loud since I was pretty sure my mom hadn't been to confession in 50 or 60 years. "That's nice of you, Father…Father?"

"Monsignor Mayweather," he corrected me. "And you are?"

"I'm Lucy's son, Doug."

"Bless you my son. Mothers are so very precious. As you know, the Lord our savior chose to put himself into the watchful hands of a human mother. Every act of mothering recollects Mary's nurturing of Jesus Christ."

I nearly let loose a *Jesus Christ* myself. Couldn't Monsignor intruder see the tears in my eyes, feel the pain in my heart?

"Your mother is a lovely woman," he added, his voice soft, flat. He looked how I'd once imagined Ichabod Crane, his big Adam's apple bobbing above his white clerical collar, a loose, lanky frame barely filling his long dark clothes. Maybe he was Ichabod Crane? Paying a visit to us here in sleepy hollow?

"I'll come back another time," he added. Why was I suddenly frightened?

The monsignor slid away from the door, turned, stopped, turned back around, and pushed his front foot into the doorway.

"Let us pray," his voice was at a different level. From somewhere he'd produced a silk, liturgical scarf in his left hand and began a blessing with his right. "God, whose word suffices to make all things holy, pour out your blessing on Lucy's home and grant her, her son Douglas, and all who enter, health in body and protection of soul by calling on your holy name; through Christ our Lord."

He looked at me and waited. Even though I had abandoned God, or vice versa, in the jungles of Vietnam almost 50 years before, I uttered "amen," for my mother. Sure she didn't go to church or confession, but Lucy still gave up candy every Lent and knelt down beside her bed and prayed every night. For me and Ron and our families. Every damn night.

Until now.

"Amen," I said louder this time, but the monsignor was gone. His words and blessing seemed to fill the tiny apartment. Had something happened, anything changed? All I knew, it was getting late, the overnight caretaking staff would be here soon, and I'd go home to spend another restless night, tossing and turning, worrying about my mom. Dreaming about Ichabod Crane, Bram Bones, and the headless horseman…

The more I thought about it, the more I decided to add the Monsignor to the mystery as well. With Father Paul as the story's hero, why not make Monsignor Mayweather the villain?

chapter six

"...Go Marching In"

None of the days on my mom's death watch were fun or easy, but weekends were the worst. Maybe that was because they *were* weekends, and we'd been conditioned over time to expect something different, brighter, better? Not now and not at All Saints. The whole place was a lot quieter, almost tomb-like; the pious, sunny staff weren't so visible; the Saturday-Sunday hospice nurses that called on Lucy less rosy and reliable; Liz's scheduling more haphazard, resulting in the two of us often tag teaming both days. Thank god Liz took the overnights, because my body and my allergies couldn't have handled another sleepover in my mom's itchy apartment.

Lucy didn't seem to enjoy weekends that much either, hankering for the good old days of large and loud Sunday night Euchre extravaganzas where she often won money. Plus, Sunday was the one day when she would usually eat a "big" breakfast—eggs or pancakes or waffles with sausage, packaged and prepared by Jimmy Dean or Roy Rogers or some other wild west cowboy entrepreneur—instead of her customary bowl of shredded wheat, glass of cranberry juice, and piece of toast. But this Sunday's Lucy Bradley menu, similar to Monday through Saturday, featured ice chips and water.

But who's fault was that anyway? No one told her she had to stop eating. She didn't have to want to die. But here we were, starving, waiting…waist deep in the big muddy.

Sunday's one redeeming virtue was the mystery show, or shows, on PBS. I couldn't tell Miss Fisher from Miss Marple, Inspector

Lewis from Inspector Morse, but my mother adored, and absorbed, those Sunday night whodunits, watching with laser-like focus. Easier now, I thought, with the TV in her bedroom.

"I can't believe how expertly your mom follows those PBS shows," our dear friend Mary marveled one night after she'd pinch hit for me so I could get some R&R—a glass of bourbon, or two—with her husband Bruce. "She fills me in on everything that's happened before and who's doing what to whom and…it's pretty amazing. She's a remarkable woman."

Indeed she is, I thought. And remarkably, she wants to die and can't.

Alas, this particular Sunday our local PBS station was holding one of its major fundraising events, an on-air auction, meaning there would be no mysteries for Lucy to unravel. All the more reason for me to bring along more book material for her to critique, if she could muster the energy.

"I missed you," my mom greeted me when I leaned down to give her a kiss. Apparently, she'd already forgotten that I'd spent most of the morning with her, and half of yesterday too. At least by now I didn't try to correct her or act bothered.

"I missed you too, Mom. How you feeling?"

"Tired of being tired." She tried to smile but couldn't. "And my shows aren't on tonight."

"Not to worry," I smiled, placing several pages of *Saints and Sinners* beside her pillow. "We can manufacture our own mystery."

Her eyes closed, her skin turned darker grey, her body heaved. For a moment, I thought I'd lost her. Then she placed her hand on mine.

"Thank you sweetie," she whispered.

"Do you remember where we left off?"

My mom gave me the kind of perturbed look she did when I was a little boy and tried, unsuccessfully, to pull something over on her.

"I'm disappointed and tired, but I'm not dead." She frowned at me as if to prove her point. "Father Paul and Chief Williams were going to investigate what was happening in Apartment 159 at All Saints."

Bingo, she's on her game. "I'm calling it Old Saints in the story, but we can call it All Saints if you want."

"Read."

"Just before Father Paul's arrival, Old Saints property manager Peggy Miller had been checking out the emergency light blinking outside Apartment 159. Using her passkey, Peggy did a quick survey of the cluttered apartment, taking some small pleasure that its owner, Bessie Procter, had recently been transferred to the long-term care unit next door."

My mom raised an index finger.

"What is it?"

You're using my apartment number."

"So what?"

"If anybody reads this, they'll know…maybe they'll worry about me."

"Mom, nobody's going to read this. Hell, we've hardly started."

"But, if we do, finish I mean, then you'll be sure and change the apartment number?"

"Okay."

"Promise me." She pinched my hand.

"Mom, I promise that I'll change the number of the apartment."

"And who's Bessie?"

"The old woman who used to live in 159. She's in a pickle, as you would say."

"Oh dear," she smiled. "I'm glad it wasn't me."

"Once she got this ungodly mess cleaned up, Peggy could turn over the keys to a new tenant and enjoy the satisfaction of once again having a completely full building—180 apartment units, 300 cranky senior citizens, and lord knows how many plenary indulgences. The tuna munchers at the diocese would heap enormous amounts of praise—but no raise— on her when she reported that good financial news. God loves a profit…"

This time, instead of a raised finger, I got a tug on my t-shirt.

"You can't say that," my mom scowled.

"Say what?"

"All that stuff about tuna munchers and profits."

"Why not?"

"It's not nice, and it's not fair." She gave me a disappointing look. "You know better."

"Mom, it's a story, it's fiction…F-I-C-T-I-O-N. And we're just starting. Let's see where this goes, if it goes anywhere. We can always go back and make changes."

"That's the second time you've been dismissive."

Jesus, now she's using big words. And we're down that old rabbit hole again, arguing about…what were we arguing about?

"Dismissive? Of what?"

"Our mystery. First you said nobody would read it. Then you said it wouldn't go anywhere." She looked hurt.

"Mom, I was just having a little fun, okay? Otherwise why bother?"

She began to open her mouth, but I kept talking so we wouldn't spend the next ten minutes fixated on the word *bother*.

"What I'm saying is, if I'm going to do this and keep my wits about me, I need a little humor or irony or whatever now and then. Nothing has to stay in. Understand?"

"Yes, dear. Thank you."

"Where were we?"

"Apartment 159."

"Peggy flipped off the emergency light, making a mental note to have her handyman Nick check into it the next day when she spotted lights in the front parking lot. Peggy picked up her pace once she realized that one of them was a police car! She checked her pager. Why no word from Joe and Helen, her resident managers. "What was all the commotion about?" she muttered to herself as she kept on moving…"

★★★

"Mom, I just inserted another bunch of asterisks to signal a break in the action."

No response.

"Mom, did you hear me? I'm shifting the scene here."

"Yes, yes I got it." She sounded less than happy. "Peggy is really Katie, isn't she?" Katie was the All Saints manager when my folks moved in here 12 years ago.

"That's right," I paused. "Is that okay? I didn't use her real name."

"No, no that's fine. But you could call her Katie if you want since nobody's going to read this anyway."

Back to our old games of gotcha. Maybe my mother was going to live forever after all…

"Margaret 'Peggy' Miller had been running Old Saints since it first opened its doors three years ago. But on nights like these— when she was tending to emergencies and roaming the halls at all hours—it seemed more like thirty.

"These old people," she'd complain to her husband Bob whenever she saw him, which wasn't that often since Bob had decided to move back to their home in Green Bay and leave Peggy here to manage the property by herself…"

"How did you know that?" came that familiar, questioning voice.

"Know what?"

"That Peggy or Katie or whoever's husband didn't live at All Saints."

"She must've mentioned that to me and Pam once."

"You've always had a good memory," she paused and smiled. "I like what you're doing with Katie's story."

"You mean Peggy?"

"Who?"

"In our story, Katie's name is Peggy."

"Oh." Another faint smile. "Is there more?"

"'It makes me feel old to be living with a bunch of senior citizens," Bob admitted to Peggy.

"Bob, you are old," Peggy pointed out to her 60-something husband.

"Okay, but I don't have to be reminded of it every day," he shot back.

Peggy wouldn't admit it because she missed Bob and she was mad at him for leaving, but he was right. Old Saints did age you, and Peggy was feeling a lot older than her 55 years tonight. And while she knew in her heart that she loved all the residents and that the Christian thing to do was to help them in every way she could, lord knows they sure made it hard sometimes. Too hard in fact. Which is why she was starting to contemplate an exit strategy..."

I looked up to see Lucy fast asleep. But when I kissed her hand, one eye opened.

"Whatever it is you're doing, I like it." She patted my hand. "With Peggy I mean. It's the same sort of thing you did with Father Paul. The behind the black story…I feel like I know them as people. And I'm curious about what'll happen to all of them."

My whole body smiled. Somewhere Stevie Wonder was singing "for once in my life."

chapter seven

Cat's Pajamas

Thanks to Liz and her staff, and the hospice nurses too, I rarely had to clean up after, or change, my mom. I hated to admit that, but it didn't seem right to see her body that way, to see her slipping away and falling apart. Or to embarrass her, and me, by having to clean her up after an accident. Sure, there were times when I was the last man standing, and I'd have to step up and do the cleaning and changing, but most days I didn't have to, and I think that was better for both of us.

I'd even leave the room when Lucy's regular "restoration" would occur. Every time I re-entered her bedroom afterwards, she would be glowing, oh so glad to be clean and comfortable, often decked out in one of the multi-colored night gowns she loved, her hair combed, looking almost like the person she used to be.

"Hi Mom," I'd smile and lean over to give her a kiss. "How are you feeling?"

"Like the cat's pajamas," she grinned as best she could.

I smiled back and squeezed her hand. Often, within minutes, she would fall asleep, worn out from all the turning and moving and effort of getting out of soiled clothing, sponged bathed, dried, oiled and lotioned, and dressed. And on every occasion she would say she felt like the cat's pajamas.

I never gave the saying much thought—my folks had lots of expressions and phrases that were unique to them, more my dad's than hers. He'd call bosses and guys who were in charge a *"big mahoff*" and utter "*elegant sufficiency*" at the end of a good meal. "*I'll fix your feet,*" he'd threaten when he'd tease you about getting even. Lucy was pretty much relegated to *cat's pajamas* and *bee's knees* kinds of stuff. I asked her once what cat's pajamas meant, and she paused for a very long time, looking deep in thought. Then she shook her head, claiming she didn't know the answer. Part of me thought it might've been a compliment she got from her much older brothers and sisters who probably grew up during the flapper era. Maybe Mary, her oldest sister, was a wannabe flapper? Alas, more Basile riddles I'd never solve.

Ah, but the real cat in pajamas was soon to make an appearance and Lucy's passage would take another detour…

★★★

My mom's one-bedroom apartment was situated at the end of a very, very long hallway. Meaning it always took a visitor a long time to get from the front door entrance after they'd dialed up and gained access to her place to eventually arrive. Plus, given the distance and twists and turns, callers would occasionally give up, or else call my cell for assistance. That happened this afternoon when Liz called to tell me that the cat lady was about ready to give up.

"Tell me again who's here?" I asked.

"The Paws for a Cause lady, remember? Lucy loves cats, is always talking about them, so I found one."

"One cat to do what?" I still wasn't getting it.

"To visit your mom. There were tons of visitation dogs but very few cats, and I'm happy to say I found one that was available."

"Available like when?"

"Now, silly. She's here, or I should say they're here, so I need you to go to the front door and show them how to get to the apartment."

After a quick check on my always-resting mom, I headed down the hall. *What was it with my mom and cats?* I wondered as I walked. I remember her pestering and pleading with my dad to get her a Siamese cat after they'd seen one in *Bell, Book, and Candle*, a

Jimmy Stewart-Kim Novak rom com. Ron and I named her Chanda and like most stuck-up cats, Chanda paid us no attention, except when we were sick and she'd rest on our chests and lick off the BenGay Lucy had applied to our foreheads to cut a fever. Otherwise, Chanda would cozy up exclusively to my mom and purr and rub against her whenever she wanted food or a favor. Turns out I was probably allergic to cats, but we didn't know very much about allergies back then.

Once Chanda was no more, she was followed by a litany of female Siamese cats, each one bigger and snobbier and meaner than the last, Missy being the worst of them. Thank God Missy had to stay behind in Philadelphia when we moved my folks to Wisconsin since cats weren't allowed in the wing of the All Saints building they were living in. I didn't have the heart to tell them that I got the call from the animal rescue place in Philly telling me that they had to "put Missy down" because no one wanted her and she was scratching and clawing any cat or person who came her way.

I was ruminating about all this and more when I turned one of the hallway corners and ran straight into a woman pushing a stroller.

"Sorry," I muttered as I stepped aside.

"Are you Doug?" the nondescript woman asked me.

"Who's asking?" I was on a mission and wasn't in the mood for small talk.

"I'm Alice. Liz, your mom's caregiver called me. We're here to see her."

I was just beginning to question why Alice would bring a baby to see my mother when she patted the top of the stroller and announced. "And this is Zeus."

Stunned, I looked down into the stroller and peered into the mesh covering to see the largest cat ever. Zeus indeed. The Greek god of sky and thunder had nothing on this creature.

"Lead the way," Alice sing-songed and off we went.

I had to admit that Lucy genuinely enjoyed the visit from Zeus, although I worried at times Zeus would cause the bed to collapse, or devour my tiny mother. Zeus wasn't just big, he had the largest head I'd ever seen on any cat or dog. He didn't do much except sit on the bed, but surprisingly, that was all my mom seemed to need.

I wasn't there the other time Zeus paid Lucy a visit. Paid being the operative word since I had no idea what this was costing. Liz just sort of offhandedly mentioned one day that Zeus was sick and couldn't visit any more. Maybe the Greeks had called him back to Mount Olympus? Or he'd gotten too large for the stroller?

Or had simply outgrown his cat's pajamas?

chapter eight

In Dreams

If the days felt as if they were all one and the same for me, a groundhog day for the dying, than I could only imagine what they were like for my mom. Was it Sunday or Tuesday? April or June? Spring or summer? 1919 or 2018? Once all the out-of-town family visitors and their attendant hubbub departed, the tedium and monotony took hold, and the only thing we could do was mange it as best we could.

Or stop.

Which is what Lucy wanted to do but it wasn't happening. I had to admit that during those moments when she was distressed and depressed she was still alive, I wished we lived in a death-with-dignity state like Oregon or Washington and she'd be permitted to take her leave. But we were stuck in a tiny apartment in Madison, Wisconsin, and we had to wait patiently for death to come calling.

Meanwhile, I had to remove my head from my ass and do a better job of keeping my mom's spirits lifted even if she couldn't get her spirit to ascend into heaven. That was job number one that bright June morning, and after she rang her bell to summon me into her bedroom, I entered with ice chips, smiles—and flowers!

"Hi Mom, it's a beautiful day! These are for you!"

"I'm still here," she muttered dejectedly, "why am I still here?

"To get flowers from me and Pam. Perk up. Let me get these in water and put them on your nightstand."

"No, wait, don't leave," she added as forcefully as she could. "I have to tell you about this dream I had just now. Maybe you can help me figure out what it means."

"Sure, Mom, whatever you need," I smiled, although I was a little skeptical since I didn't recall us ever going over a dream of hers. But, since we were in unchartered territory, why not go all in?

"What was the dream about?"

"It was very vivid," she began. "I was back in our big house on 47th Street in Philadelphia where I grew up. But I wasn't a little girl, I was me, now. None of my brothers and sisters were around, but Mom and Pop were somewhere in the house…"

"And?"

"Where was I?"

"In your house at 47th Street."

"Yes. There was knock on the door, and before I could get there to open it, in came this long, long line of priests."

"Priests?" Had she been conscious during Monsignor Mayweather's visit?

"Yes, a long line of priests and they all looked exactly the same."

"How so?"

"Very tall, grey hair, big eyes, long necks, white collars, long, black cassocks and…"

"And what?"

"They were all wearing snowshoes! And as they slid across the floor, they made this swooshing sound. Like there was snow on the floor. They were coming toward me, the swooshes getting louder and closer and…"

"Then what?"

"I woke up." She seemed disappointed. "What do you think it all means?"

"Hmm, not sure. What do *you* think it means?"

"I'm going to die, of course. But why a long line of priests. And the snowshoes?"

"You got me."

"You're no help."

"Sorry, Mom, but, like you, I'm guessing the priests are probably coming to give you last rites, but I don't have any idea why they're wearing snowshoes."

A long pause. "Do you think we should put that in the story?"

"The dream?"

"Sure. Maybe you could make it a dream Father Paul has, some kind of clue to his solving the mystery."

"If that's what you want, sure."

"On second thought." She was obviously plotting this out in her head. "Maybe don't put it in. Put a dream in there if you want, but not that dream."

"Anything you say, Mom."

"Thanks, sweetie. Now get those lovely flowers in some water. And thank Pam for me."

Heading to the kitchen to look for a vase, I thought about the priest's visit of a few days before, how my mother may have heard him, how there'd been a line of All Saints folks outside her door to visit her before I put a stop to it. That explained some of the dream, but the snowshoes?

"Beautiful." My mom smiled when I placed the vase next to her bed, the functional hospice hospital bed, not the nice new one Pam and I just bought for her a few months earlier. This thing didn't quite fit with the rest of her bedroom décor.

"I'll ask Liz about my dream," she said.

"Why Liz?"

"Don't you think she's in tune with things like that? She looks the part. No wonder she's a death ruler."

"Doula."

"Hula?"

"No, mom, Liz is a *death doula*. That's how she refers to herself."

Lucy burst out laughing, laughter I hadn't heard come out of her in days.

"What's so funny?"

"That's such a funny job title, don't you think? Even if I had it wrong, I was afraid to ask because it sounded so strange. But what does a death doer do anyway?"

"Death doulas help people at the end of their life with dying."

"Really? Then why isn't she helping me?"

"She is, Mom. Liz and her team are wonderful, loving caregivers. Liz knows when and how death comes. She'll help you and us be ready for it."

"Well I'm ready, so tell her to try a little harder. Or pay her less if it isn't happening."

I wasn't going to sit there and try to explain that wasn't how it works and that Liz was damn good at what she does, etc.

"Time to rest. Hospice will be here soon for your sponge bath and change. Liz will stop by later. When she does, ask her about the dream."

"What dream?"

"The one about you and the priests. The snowshoes."

"Well, if Liz is as good as you say, she should know all about that already, don't you think?"

chapter nine
We Are Family

My mother's reverie prompted me to look hard, again, at the family portrait that stood proudly on her dresser. Was this photograph really almost 100 years old? And all the subjects dead? What did I really know about any of them? And what grip did they have on my 99 year-old mother?

The more I looked, the more I wondered. And then I counted. The total should have been 13—two parents and 11 offspring—but it was 14. What the heck…? And then I remembered that my dying mother, only recently, explained that Henry Basile, her father Giuseppe's brother, lived with them back then. Little Lucy, being the last of the Basile children, was situated, more like pinned, between her oldest sister and mother, most likely because she was squirming. I closed my eyes and imagined those people, that day, my mother at three years of age, and I fell asleep…

I awoke in a startle, loud banging on the apartment door, my mother excitedly ringing her bell. I jumped to the door first where a new young, wet-behind-the-ears hospice caretaker smiled and I motioned her to come in. Then to my mom who was…asleep? Wasn't she just ringing that damn bell? Or was that part of the dream?

★★★

Back home later, exhausted, bewildered, uneasy about my mom's situation, I started to write about the dream I'd had earlier. Nothing like my mom's with the priests and the snowshoes…no, it was as if she was talking to me, telling me a story. About that day.

In the course of the dream conversation, my mom went from being her 99-year-old dying self to the three-year-old little girl in the photo. Initially, she used the term *"epiphany,"* one of my favorite words, to describe her memory of that day. But then she smiled, explaining that *epiphany* didn't capture all that it was.

"That's part of my problem," she laughed, "one that stems from nine decades of doing crossword puzzles. There has to be one perfect word that fits just right. The exact word. But it escapes me…"

And then the older Lucy went on to say the photo may have been the last time all the Basiles were gathered as one family. "All 13 of us, plus Uncle Henry," she pointed at the portrait, "beginning with Mom and Pop and ending with me. Before marriages and grandchildren."

Then the three-year-old Lucy was giggling, explaining how she had to be propped up on a table between her mother Maria and her oldest sister Mary.

"Look closer," she urged me. "See how Mom's got her hand on my left leg, trying to make me stop jiggling it, and Mary's elbow is pushing down on my other leg. Silly little girl!"

Then Lucy turns 99 again. "As I look back on it, I recall the pain in both my legs, my wanting to holler, 'Owwww' or shout, 'That hurts.' But I didn't, because I knew I'd get far worse if I didn't just settle down and shut my trap, as my brother Vince cautioned me."

And then both Lucys blended together in two-part harmony, pointing out that her oldest brother Clarence was back from winning World War I, her other older brothers were all dressed to the nines… yet all of them looking as if they were mad about something.

And then a voice came from somewhere else. My father's? It kept repeating how the right word to describe that moment was crucial. Happiness, sadness, pain, fear, pleasure, hope…what was it about that moment?

In bed later that night, I flashed back to the dream, hoping I could find the key to what my mother was trying to tell me. Did she foresee then that eventually things would go wrong? That something would happen—the Great Depression, World War II, her father's illness, other family drama—that would tear her family apart at the seams?

I smiled as I thought about it, how *seams* was a perfect metaphor for a big Italian family whose patriarch was a tailor. But did they really come apart at the seams? Maybe that's the word Lucy was looking for…Things weren't what they seemed, even back then and now she's the only one left to tell the story.

And now it's up to me to help her to do that. I'm her medium. *We'll get to that next,* I promised the dark. *Once little Lucy and I have completed* Saints and Sinners, *we'll dig deep into the Basile family and write that story too.*

Assuming, of course, that my mom will be around that long. Given how things are going, that's a definite possibility.

chapter ten

Strike One

As I mentioned, All Saints Apartment 159 sat at the end of a very, very long hallway. Really long. The good news was the trek served as Lucy's workout routine during the nine years she lived there. She made that trip at least three times a day—to fetch her newspaper, to get her mail, or go to chair exercises, euchre, pinochle, Wii bowling, or whatever. The bad news is that nurses and caregivers and case workers and all the rest who came to see her would sometimes get lost, a la Alice and Zeus, or else give up, as they tried to wend their way to the very distant apartment numbered 159.

My solution was to let those folks into the complex via the side door downstairs that was adjacent to the parking lot. Way easier. But this was not the "official" way in and out of the All Saints compound—the downstairs door had a sign with big letters declaring "EMERGENCY EXIT. THIS IS NOT AN ENTRANCE." You couldn't enter the building from there, key or no key, so my solution was to prop the door open, usually with one of my mother's many shoes or shoe boxes, when I knew Liz or hospice or someone else would be arriving. Of course, my contrary, against-the-rules, approach drew criticism, censure, and, literally, damnation, from the All Saints residents and staff. My rule breaking must have been akin to having committed a mortal sin.

No sooner had I escorted Brandy, one of our favorite overnight sitters, down the stairs and out the unauthorized door, than one of the first floor cranks spied me through their curtains, wagged a finger and shouted, "You can't use that door."

I smiled politely, mouthing the words, "I just did."

Of course, later I would get a call or a visit from the resident staff reminding me not to do that again. Another order which I'd ignore. Didn't they realize I wasn't breaking the rules just to break them, but that my 99 year-old mother was dying and using this damn door made things easier for her? For us? Why didn't that predicament appeal to their Catholic charity?

I was surprised to hear my mom ringing her little bell when I got back to her apartment.

"Hi Mom, you're up early."

"Guess what Liz said?"

"About what?"

"About my dream, silly."

"The one with the priests and the snowshoes?"

"Yes. Liz agrees with us about why the priests are coming to see me. She thinks there's a line of them—she guessed maybe there were nine or ten—to represent the decades of my life."

"Okay."

"And she knew all about what snow means. I told you she was into stuff like that."

I smiled, knowing that the Lucy vs. Doug tally had just added one for her. For all I knew, she was keeping score.

"So what about the snow and the snowshoes?"

"Liz says that snow often represents death. But dreaming about snow can sometimes mean that a stage in your life is over and a new beginning is coming."

"But isn't this more of an ending than a beginning?" I hadn't caught myself before those words came out.

"Of course." She wasn't the least bit chagrined. "I'm at the end. The end of the beginning. That's what the snow means." She seemed very sure of herself.

"And the snowshoes?"

She laughed. "Have you seen my closet? Liz calls me a clothes whore. But I've got way more shoes than clothes. You even counted them once—weren't there 40 or 50 shoe boxes in there?"

"Mom, I think Liz said you were a clothes *horse*, not whore. And yes, you've got more shoes than Imelda Marcos."

"Who?"

"Doesn't matter. So the priests wear snowshoes because there's snow and you have lots of shoes in your closet?"

"Exactly."

"Okay, so basically your dream means you're going to receive the last rites from a priest and then die. And soon?"

"I hope so." She let out a deep sigh. "Bring me some ice chips please and then close the curtains. I need to rest."

"I brought along more of the story when you're ready," I told her when I reentered the bedroom.

"Goodie," she smiled faintly. "Let's do that after I wake up…if I wake up."

I never told her about my dream. And what we would do after we were done with the *Saints and Sinners* story we were working on…

★★★

After the hospice nurse and the sponge bath and the bedding and nightgown change and all the rest, the sun was dipping low and soon I'd be heading home. I kept bedside vigil watching Lucy sleep and twitch and, at times, appear to have stopped breathing. Liz told us this was normal for a person who was approaching death.

"It's called *Cheyne-Stokes* breathing," she explained one afternoon over coffee in my mom's cramped kitchen. "Sometimes the breathing deepens. Sometimes it speeds up. And sometimes it's so shallow that you think it's stopped."

"Does it follow a pattern?" I asked. "Can you gauge how close someone is to dying by their breathing rhythms?"

Liz smiled. "It's different for everyone." She paused, placing her consoling hand on top of mine. "If you're wondering where Lucy is with all this, it's hard to say. It's coming. She's getting closer, but we don't know if it'll be tomorrow or the next day or…"

"Or next week? Or the week after?" I exchanged a pained look with Pam.

"Lucy's doing this her way, and we just have to let it take its course."

As I recalled this conversation and watched my mom for telltale signs, she opened her eyes.

"What did I miss?" she asked.

"You didn't miss anything, Mom." I squeezed her hand and smiled.

"But aren't you reading our story?"

"I haven't started yet."

"Well, start now." She swiveled her shoulders in an attempt to sit up in bed. "I'm ready."

★★★

"Lost in her thoughts, Peggy noticed that her pager was vibrating. "Alpha numeric my butt," she grumbled aloud, recalling the tutorial she'd attended on the device last month. Peggy loved her cell phone but couldn't get any reception inside the Old Saints labyrinth, hence the need for pagers. The latest gizmos were able to receive text messages through email, or via the Holy Ghost, so this was probably from Joe and Helen telling her that the police were on the premises. Duh, *she thought.*

But when she looked down, the message read "Dearie, you left the light on," and it was signed "Apartment 159."

Confused, and a little frightened, Peggy decided NOT to walk back in the direction of Apartment 159, but instead she walked briskly toward the main entrance. But what was that noise behind her? She was wondering about that and the light in apartment 159 when she looked up to see her favorite priest, Father Paul, and another man she didn't recognize, standing in the main entrance.

"Father Paul, what brings you here on this dark and stormy night," Peggy smiled, sharing an inside joke with her old friend. She and Father Paul used to swap the world's worst "dark and stormy

night" sentences for laughs. They'd even entered a few of their own into the annual Bulwer-Lytton competition.

"Evening, ma'am." The other man tipped his hat and addressed her. Peggy didn't realize he was talking to her until she was looking straight at him.

"Peggy, this is Chief Williams," Father Paul interrupted. He touched her small, stubby hand and placed it between his.

"Hello, Peggy." Chief Williams extended his hand. Peggy dropped her hand from Father Paul's and shook Melvin's vigorously. Melvin smiled.

"I sure hope my old friend here is a better priest than he was a detective," Melvin said with a straight face.

Peggy already liked the detective's demeanor, but her old friend didn't appear to be the least bit amused.

"Peggy, I had a call tonight about an emergency here at Old Saints." Father Paul commanded her attention.

"If you tell me it has something to do with Apartment 159, I'm going to start saying the rosary right here," Peggy smiled.

"Blessed be God, Peggy, it was Apartment 159!" the priest erupted.

"What in the hell are we waiting for?" shouted Chief Williams. "Peggy, what's the quickest way to 159?"

"Follow me." The three of them charged off."

"Why did you stop?" my mom asked.

"I thought you were asleep."

"Just resting my eyes," she explained. "This part's pretty good, but I think you've slowed down the action too much. And it's a little confusing. Where are Father Paul and Chief Williams exactly?"

"In the front lobby of All Saints."

"Still?"

"Sure. Don't you remember? Father Paul got hit on the head and Chief Williams came to his aid."

"Yes I remember alright, but where's his car? And who left the light on in my apartment?"

"That's part of the mystery, Mom. And don't worry about the setting. You know this place too well, so try to not be so critical. Pretend you're somewhere else."

"I wish I were somewhere else," she added, pointing upwards toward her ceiling, the All Saints roof above it, and, at the very top, her eventual heavenly home.

"Are we done for today?" I asked.

She made a turning notion with her hand that directed me to keep going.

"The trio walked swiftly and silently down two long corridors of shiny new apartment entrances adorned with crucifixes, portraits of the virgin mother, and smiley faces. They zipped past an elevator and the laundry room, turned a corner, and encountered a bright, flashing white light. The door to Apartment 159 was wide open.

Inside they found the apartment's previous occupant, Bessie Proctor, seated at a table in her kitchen nook. In front of her was the weekly score sheet summary from the Old Saints Wii bowling league. Bessie's white hair was parted down the middle and she had a vacant look in her eyes. She also had a thin knife sticking through her tiny neck. Above it, on her forehead, written in red magic marker were the words, "Strike one."

"Oh, that's good." Lucy perked up. "Now this is getting interesting."

The knock on her front door made us both jump. Lucy gave me a look as if to say, "Can't we keep going?" But it was time for me to go.

"I'm glad you like it, Mom. I'll bring more tomorrow. Keep thinking about what you want to have happen next. And who the murderer might be."

"Maybe the murderer's at my door." She gave me a slight smile, then reached out and grabbed my hand. "Thanks, sweetie. See you tomorrow unless…"

"I'll see you tomorrow, Mom. Have a good night," I said and then went to greet her overnight caregiver. Or maybe Monsignor Mayweather would be standing at her door? Could *he* be the murderer?

chapter eleven

Breaking and Entering

Everything remained just as it was. Lucy spent most of her time sleeping. Ice chips, sponge baths, and brief conversations her only waking interludes. And, of course, complaining. Oh, and her PBS mysteries on Saturday and Sunday nights. With the TV in her bedroom, my mom could watch in relative comfort, the sound turned low but the captions writ large.

"Don't you just love Miss Fisher?" Lucy would pose this question every week during an episode of *Miss Fisher's Murder Mysteries*.

"Yeah, she's pretty good," I'd reply, not paying attention to the televised goings-on.

"No, I mean, don't you think she's cute?" My mom would smile, imagining my harboring a secret crush for the 1920s TV sleuth. And then she'd lie back, close her eyes, and for all I know became Miss Fisher herself.

Sunday's *Masterpiece* mysteries were even better, so I wouldn't bother bringing sections of my mediocre mystery for us to work on, knowing whatever I'd written would pale in comparison. In fact, I started to stay away longer on the weekends, even if it was costing us with Liz and her caregivers. I needed the break and cherished the 48 hours when I didn't have to email and text hospice and Liz and CARE Wisconsin, the state Medicaid plan which was turning out to be way more trouble and expense than it was worth. None of these agencies checked in with one another, so it was my job to keep them on the same page regarding my mom's status.

Which, day in and day out, week in and week out, was always the same old song—no food, no headway, no exit for little Lucy. So, no wonder I was startled to find her sitting up in bed looking like the cat who ate the canary when I stopped by this sunny June morning after my "48-hour weekend pass."

"Mom, hi…you're…up?"

"Yes I am. Have been. Where were you all weekend?"

I sputtered, trying to come up with some lame excuse when one of the several hospice nurses named Megan entered the room with a tray that had toast, cheese, and fruit on it. I quickly put up my hands and ushered Megan back out of the room.

"Mom, what the hell? *You're eating?"* I was incredulous.

"I guess I am," she replied sheepishly.

"Since when? What the hell's going on?" I was done being touchy-feely with her. "You don't eat for 30 days."

"Thirty-three," she corrected me.

"Thirty-three goddamn days," my voice was rising, "and all of a sudden you're going to start eating again? After you stopped eating and said you wanted to die? What the hell, Lucy!"

My mother winced. I could see a startled Megan in my mom's doorway.

"Please don't be mad at your mom." She walked to the side of Lucy's bed as if to protect her from my words. "It was my fault. A couple of her friends brought her a tray of food from some party on Saturday. I didn't see them bring it in, and before I knew it they were gone and your mother had a tummy ache."

"No shit," I snorted.

"Douglas!" My mother's voice hadn't sounded this strong in weeks. Maybe it was the food? "No more swearing. Inky and Sally were at Deb's going away party and they wanted me to see what had been served. Megan didn't see them come in. Vicki, one of Liz's girls was here too part of the time. Inky and Sally kinda snuck in. If it's anybody's fault, it's mine."

"She threw most of it up," Megan chimed in. I turned in her direction, more annoyed by the minute.

"So that makes it okay, does it? Damnit to hell!" This time Megan winced.

My anger and bluster had filled the room. My mom and Megan cowered, looking as if they'd been punched. I flashed back on stories my deceased dad told me of his abusive father pummeling him and his mother. Was that what I was doing?

"Sorry, Megan," I added after a long pause. "Let me talk to my mom alone please?"

Megan exited, and I sat down next to Lucy and held her hand.

"Mom, tell me why you ate the food?"

"Because it was there," she said innocently. "I hadn't thought about any food until I saw it and, well, it was better than ice chips. Chocolate cake and vanilla ice cream too!" She licked her lips.

"So, you are back to eating now?"

A long silence. I could almost hear the wheels turning.

"I don't know," she sighed. "It's not like I want to eat, but not eating doesn't seem to be getting me anywhere." Another pause. "Maybe I'm not going to die? Maybe I should just go back to living and eating."

"But Mom, you can't start eating after you've been off food for so long. And don't you remember what it was like before? You were miserable. Coughing. Throwing up. You hated it."

"But I hate this too. I just want to be done with it all."

"Me too, Mom." I stroked her hand and kept my head down. "Me, too."

If my mom's spirits hadn't been broken, mine sure as well had. Nearly five straight weeks of ice chips down the drain. And she was still here. More than here. Very, very present with her faculties. Maybe we did need to forget the whole thing? But then she wouldn't be able to stay in the apartment and the CARE folks would probably put her in assisted living someplace and…

The door to her room opened and there was Inky. How did this guy keep getting into my mom's apartment? Then I remembered we didn't lock the door so Lucy's caregivers could come and go. I was ready to let Inky have it but noticed how fragile and helpless he seemed.

"Hi Lucy," he smiled at my mom, who waved. He turned to me.

"I'm sorry." He held out his hand to mine as if to shake on it. When I reached mine back, he grabbed it, held it tightly, and started to sob.

"Lucy was such a big fan of Deb's who's been here at All Saints about as long as your mom. We knew she'd be sad if she didn't get a chance to be part of the going away festivities and…"

"But Deb and her boss have been by here a couple times to check in on my mom. They've probably said their goodbyes already." I interrupted his confession.

"But parties are different. Your mom loved every All Saints party. She'd always get introduced as our oldest resident!"

Lucy smiled at this. As angry as I was at Inky, there was something about his forlorn look that kept me from chewing him out.

"Just don't do this again without checking with me first, okay?"

"Okay," a contrite Inky nodded. Then he added, "We miss you Lucy," as he teared up and exited the room.

Poor guy, I thought, *I think he has a crush on my mother.*

After my mom dozed off, I went upstairs to Sally's apartment to set things straight with her. She hollered "come in" after I knocked. I was surprised to see her sitting in the middle of the room, surrounded by all kinds of medical equipment and space age gadgets, smoking a cigarette.

"How's Lucy?"

"Okay, thanks. But I need you to promise me that you won't bring her food any more please."

"Yeah, I guess it wasn't such a good idea was it? We just wanted her to be happy." Sally paused and pulled on her cigarette. "To tell you the truth, we really just wanted to see your mom and her smiling face." Another inhale. She cocked her head sideways so she wouldn't blow the smoke in my face. "But, sure, sorry. It won't happen again."

Sally could tell I was eying her cigarette. Smoking wasn't allowed anywhere on the All Saints premises.

"I know," she nodded. "I shouldn't be smoking. But it's my only way to cope. All this equipment is for my husband, Frank. He's asleep in the bedroom. He's dying, and there's nothing I can do."

"I'm sorry," I spoke softly. "Is there anything I can do?"

"Have your mom give him a hard time like she used to," she joked. "And if you see the Monsignor in the hallway, send him up. I don't know how much longer Frank's gonna last."

Re-entering my mom's apartment, I could hear a new female voice talking to my mom, sweetly. Today's hospice nurse must have been giving her a sponge bath because I could hear the water wringing into the basin. For some reason that made me think of my mom being baptized…or given her last rites.

"I love that nightie on you." I could hear the young woman flattering my mom. And I knew Lucy would be smiling.

All of this entering and exiting and yelling wasn't getting me anywhere. I was angry about so many things and had almost taken it out on two helpless All Saints seniors.

And on my dying mother.

As I sat there, trying to calm down, I realized Lucy would know what to do next. If she wanted to keep eating, she'd keep eating. If she didn't, well…

I needed to get my shit together. Apologize to my mom for swearing, for scaring her and Megan. I had to get back to being more upbeat. Less distracted. To connecting the Lucy-care dots among all her caregivers. To being a good son.

To get back to our All Saints mystery.

I smiled at that thought. Hell, so what if two of her biggest fans and fellow Pinochle players wanted my mom to eat? It wasn't the end of the world, was it?

No, that was something that still awaited Lucy.

But when…?

chapter twelve

Holy Rollers

Another early Monday morning hand off from Brandy. Or was it Tuesday? Didn't matter. Lucy had decided to **not** eat any more food and return to intaking ice chips on her passage to passing. But now she was suffering from very painful constipation, so I was trying to navigate between hospice who did not want my mom to have a suppository and Liz and her team who did. Seeing my mom in such discomfort, I sided with Liz. But so far nothing had happened. All the more reason to get back to our mystery and get Lucy's mind off her biological speedbumps.

"Do you remember where we left off?" I waved several pages at my mom as I pulled the desk chair next to her bed.

"What did you say to Sally?"

I pretended not to hear. "Mom, did you hear me? I've got some more excerpts to share. Do you remember where we stopped?"

"I heard you alright. But what did you say to my friends?"

"I told them both to stop bringing you food."

"But did you say it nicely?" Her accusatory tone conjured glimpses of a quivering Inky and smoking Sally.

"Mom, I'm sorry if I offended your friends. I'm not myself sometimes, okay? I'm stressed out about all this…worried to death about you. Maybe I overreacted." Suddenly I was close to tears, why I didn't know.

She patted my hand. "Tell them you're sorry. That's all." She paused looking at my handful of pages. "Now, where were we?"

"There'd been a murder and…"

"The old lady in my apartment got knifed through the throat," my mom said in a near bloodthirsty tone. No wonder she liked books like *Devil's Gambit*. "Read on Macduff," she smiled and I picked up the pages.

"Every year, just before Labor Day, the senior residents of Old Saints would come together to celebrate mass, take Holy Communion, and choose teams for its Annual Wii Bowling League. Peggy Miller established herself as league commissioner, which included compiling the weekly statistical update, settling disputes (of which there were many), and overseeing the annual player "draft." The latter placed Peggy in charge of choosing Wii bowling team captains."

My mom's hand was raised.

"What happened to the lady who was killed?"

"Whaddya mean what happened?"

"Wasn't there an investigation?"

"Sure, probably, but I wanted to shift the scene, add some comic relief by setting up the Wii bowling league since it has something to do with the murders."

"You mean there's more than one?" she piped up.

"Of course there are," I nodded, "how could a Lucy Bradley mystery have only one murder?"

She laughed but then stopped because it hurt her tummy.

"So I suppose you'll come back to that murder investigation after this?"

"For sure," I lied because today's batch of pages were as far as I'd gotten. I couldn't bring myself to write about anything other than my mom's dying. Not some stupid mystery that's for sure.

"Okay," she said. "Keep going."

"Peggy usually based her team selections on a combination of Old Saints seniority and attendance at Sunday mass, which was held

in the main lounge at 11 a.m. every Sunday, the exact same location for Wii bowling. As part of the captain selection process, Peggy also had to be sure to censor some of the proposed team names the elderly captains came up with. Just last year, she had to put the kibosh on "Bowl Movements," "Split Happens," and "Dolls with Balls," prompting Peggy to wonder just how smutty the minds of her senior inhabitants were."

I could hear Lucy muffling a laugh. "That's true you know," she giggled.

"Listen up, everybody, it's time to get started." Peggy rang the bell on the table in front of the room, now crowded with 50 or more Old Saints residents, nearly twice the number that usually attended Sunday mass. "I'll begin by naming the team captains and saying their team names," Peggy continued in a loud voice, "and they'll each choose four players for their respective teams, making one selection at a time until all the teams are filled."

"What'd she say?" hollered Marilyn Gall to anyone who'd listen.

"Which Bill?" asked Bill Dvorak from the back of the room.

"She said fill, not Bill," shot back Paulette Beyler who was still mad about losing the championship last year.

Peggy rang the bell twice. And a third time, extra loud.

"Please, everyone, just calm down and listen up. I'll go slow and one at a time." Most heads nodded in agreement. Others had already nodded off.

"First up is Merval Shaw. Her team is 'Queen Pins.' Groans emanated from a few of the men in the audience, which were quickly drowned out by the applause of Merval's cadre of girlfriends. Merval used her walker to make way to the front of the room, her Bucky Badger sweatsuit having seen better days. She was also wearing her high top sneakers.

Peggy smiled at Merval, remembering her hissy fit last year when Peggy wouldn't let her replace Oren Hempstead with Jeannette Shelly in mid-season. Jeanette was a better Wii bowler than Oren and didn't like being on Dorothy Beyler's team anyway. It wasn't her fault that Oren passed away in mid-season, and the rules are the rules, meaning that Merval had to select someone off the sub list, not from another team. Ever since, Merval had not been a happy camper."

A knock on the door and an entrance by Monday Megan. So it was Monday after all.

"Mornin' Lucy! Hi Doug! How are we doing today?"

"*We* are fine and *we* are working on our story," my mom replied through gritted teeth.

"Oh, sorry. I'm here until 1 p.m. so if you need anything let me know. Thought maybe we could have a sponge bath and a change."

"*We* might like a change and *we* will let you know," my mom nodded toward the door where Megan exited.

"Mom, be nice to Megan. She's only doing her job."

"She's always interrupting. They're all interrupting. I just get a little tired of it."

"We're all tired," I said, holding her hand. "Relax and be patient."

"But I am the patient," she winked at me. "And where did you come up with those names? They're not anyone who lives here but they're perfect Wisconsin names. I've never met so many Lyles, Norberts, and Marcellas in my life."

"It's called comic relief. Thought we'd need that after the murder."

"I could use some chronic relief," she muttered, tapping the page. "Keep going."

"As she watched Merval make her way to the front of the room, Peggy glanced down at her notes for the captains and their respective teams, whispering a little prayer that everything would go according to plan.

*Team: **Queen Pins** Captain: **Merval Shaw***

Merval came in third place last year. She's said she never wants another man on her team since the last two had died during the season. "Besides," she told Peggy, "what kind of man wants to be called a Queen anyway?"

*Team: **Lucky Strikes** Captain: **Dottie Ballweg***

Dottie's teams have landed in last place each of the past two years, but she has the best attitude and is kind to her team members. She does cheat on her scores, however, and gets mad when Peggy calls her on it.

*Team: **Spare Me** Captain: **Bill Dvorak***

This is Bill's first year here, and so far he's made a good impression, especially among the widows because he still drives a car and can walk without any assistance. For sure she won't be putting either of the two resident hussies, Shirley Meinholtz or Grace Sanders, on Bill's team!

*Team: **Alley Cats** Captain: **Allie Greenberg***

Allie has a hard time filling her roster every year because some of the Old Saints residents think she's Jewish. "My mother liked Jewish names, so she changed her name to Greenberg after my dad died," she explained to Peggy. Heck, Allie took communion every week, which was good enough for Peggy. Still, she needed to be sure to place some of the harder of hearing types on that team so they wouldn't fixate on Allie's name.

*Peggy's heart sank as she glanced down at the large stack of papers with extra sheets of paper with **six more** team names and captains. Six more!*

*Team: **The Bowling Stones** Captain: **Delmar Gest***
*Team: **Pin Pushers** Captain: **Frances Frydenlund***
*Team: **I Can't Believe It's Not Gutter** Captain: **Marilyn Gall***
*Team: **Holy Rollers** Captain: **Paulette Beyler***
*Team: **Strikes-R-Us** Captain: **Frank Worley***
*Team: **Pin Ups** Captain: **Rose Defelice"***

Not only was Lucy giggling, but so was Megan who was standing by the door.

"This is cute and really funny." Megan smiled broadly and looked down at my mom, who was trying hard not to laugh too much. She made a rotating motion with her index figure that said, "Keep going."

"This will take all day," Peggy thought to herself, already sorry she'd exercised so much control of the Wii bowling league. Who cared if a bunch of 80-somethings wanted to cheat on their scores or belittle one another? They'd have to answer to God, not to her.

Just then Peggy felt someone tugging on her sleeve and turned to see Paulette Beyler smiling. Paulette was the most pious person in Old Saints, hiring cabs to attend daily mass at Good Shepherd where Father Seamus Paul served the Lord. She was also one of the retirement community's better dressers, always decked out in dresses, heels and stockings, her white hair pulled back into a nice, tight bun.

"Excuse me, Margaret dear, but I have a suggestion," Paulette offered. She was the only Old Saints resident who called her Margaret. Peggy half-smiled because Paulette <u>always</u> had a suggestion. Meanwhile, Frank Worley was telling Rose Defelice that she couldn't pick him for her team because he was captain of his own team.

"Yes, Paulette, what is it?"

"We could count off."

"What?" Peggy wasn't sure she heard what Paulette was saying.

"We could count off." Paulette smiled her angelic smile. "We have ten teams, so we need 40 players, correct? If we all just counted off in 4s. then all the 1s would be on one team, all the 2s on another, and . .

"Paulette, dear," Peggy interrupted diplomatically. "If we did it that way, there would be 10 ones and ten twos and so on. We need ten teams of four players, not four teams of ten players.

"Oh dear," Paulette sighed.

Peggy smiled to ease Paulette's disappointment. Just as she began to place her hand on Paulette's shoulder, Peggy saw Rose Defelice swatting at Frank Worley with her rosary beads. Peggy turned and grabbed Rose's hand and stepped between her and Frank.

"Rose, please, stop it! STOP!!" Peggy grabbed Rose roughly by the wrist. Rose grimaced. Frank was sputtering.

"Never in my life." Frank was beside himself, his ample belly hanging inches below his beltline, moving dangerously close to his high black socks atop his dazzling white shoes. "That woman is dangerous!"

Groups of Old Saints residents were beginning to cluster around the two combatants. Peggy took a deep breath, quickly plotting her strategy. As she moved back to the front table to ring her bell, the fire alarm went off—a loud, pulsing beeping sound accompanied by brilliant, flashing white lights. The obedient, well-trained Old Saints residents began to make their way to the exit, one cane, one walker, and one wheelchair at a time…"

"I've laughed so hard I peed my pants," my mom volunteered.

"Let me help you with that." Megan moved toward the bed. Since I'd relinquished the job of assisting my mom with her failing bodily functions, I exited stage left.

"Is this the actual All Saints Wii bowling league you're writing about?" Megan asked innocently as I was leaving. "I overhear lots of the residents talking about it as if it was the best thing going."

"No, I made all this up," I corrected Megan. "I mean, yes, there is a Wii bowling league here, but it's not the one I'm writing about in our story."

"Who cares?" Megan giggled. "It's a hoot."

"That's my boy." Lucy smiled proudly in my direction. "Doug's a published writer you know."

chapter thirteen

Back to Basics

I wouldn't admit it to my mom, but I'd almost come to the end of what I'd written for our Old Saints, a.k.a. All Saints, mystery. She and I had embarked on this so-called collaboration nine years ago right after my dad died, but after that initial burst of expressive enthusiasm neither of us had done much to move things along, me writing-wise and Lucy editing and advising-wise. Not to mention whether or not the mystery we were creating was any good, my mom's recent tributes notwithstanding.

As a result, I turned to the members of my longstanding writing group, the Deadly Writers Patrol, for feedback. Minus interruptions of course. DWP, as we referred to ourselves, was comprised of a motley assortment of Vietnam veteran would-be authors, a young Iraqi war vet poet, and a veteran-oriented UW prof who cared deeply about us vets and our issues. And who himself had written several non-fiction books about race and music. The Old Saints mystery excerpts I read to DWP were unlike anything I'd written about the war, its haunting legacies, and post-Vietnam America. My fellow DWPers, supportive and sympathetic as always, were less than enthusiastic about the mystery I was trying to write.

"Why again are you writing this?" asked Bruce, a fellow rear echelon soldier in Vietnam.

"Because my mom loves mysteries and has read almost all of them, and I thought we'd have fun doing this together and…"

"But is she *doing* any of it? Or is it all you? And a mystery? Really?"

"Has your mother read any Louise Penny?" interjected Steve, a bearded vet who witnessed way too much ugliness in 'Nam as a 19 year-old. Steve seemed eager to change the subject.

"Come again?"

"Get your mom some Louise Penny mysteries. Great stuff. She's a Canadian author whose Quebec inspector Armand Gamache is terrific."

"Okay," I demurred, "but what about this story I'm writing. Is it any good?"

Silence.

★★★

I wasn't looking forward to confessing my manuscript misdemeanors to my mom, but there was no way I could continue this story, *her* story, without more of her input and insights. I'd hit a high point with the Wii bowling episode, but that was the last thing I'd put together. I needed her to tell me where to go from here. And how to get there.

Given Lucy's weakening condition, I wondered whether she'd even notice if I re-read the excerpts I'd already shared with her? No sooner did that thought cross my mind than I realized:

1. If anyone would know I was simply rewinding the same scenarios, it would be my mother;

2. By doing that, I would disappoint the hell out of her by not following through on my promise.

And

3. Lucy would be even madder at me for trying to pull something over on her.

Now that we were waist deep in the fifth week of my mom's declining spiral, I felt caught between an unstoppable force—death—and an unmovable object—my mother. With no way out, in reality or in fiction.

But just as those doors were closing…

I could hear my mom talking with another of the new hospice nurses. Their names and faces and shifts varied a lot, which, oddly, was turning out to be a good thing because it forced my mom to engage and be sociable every time she'd meet somebody new. And, like today, when one of the newbies, as my mom called them, was changing her bedding or bathing her or gently applying lotion to her weakened frame, they'd have these nice conversations about Lucy's life and her marriage to my dad and, mostly, about her big Italian family.

"How many brothers and sisters did you have Lucy?" asked one of today's Megans or Carlas or Robyns on the hospice team.

"Six brothers and four sisters." I could almost hear her smile. "We had so much fun together. I loved being a part of that big, loud, happy family."

"So did you and your husband have lots of kids?"

"We couldn't," her voice weakened. "I had a hysterectomy after Doug was born. So we only had two."

"But two good sons, I bet," came the nurse's polite response. Was the sound I thought I heard my mom's feeble head nodding?

"You'd like Ron, Doug's older brother. He's lots of fun." A long pause. "They're different. Doug is more like his father."

"When did your husband pass?"

"Nine years ago. Prostate cancer finally got him."

"I'm so sorry."

"It's okay. He was almost 90. He had a good life. At least his 67 years with me," she laughed. "He used to say he wouldn't live to be 50. Boy was he ever wrong."

A slight titter from her caretaker.

"Was he in World War II?"

"Yep," my mom offered. "But Doug was in Vietnam," she paused for emphasis, "and that was really something!"

"Thank you for your service," the nurse said awkwardly when I reentered the room. Even in her frail state, my mom looked like a new person. Clean. Refreshed. Smiling.

"I like her," my mom said as the nurse exited. "Poor thing. She's a single parent and has to drop her little boy off at her mother's every time she's on call. What a shame."

"You two seemed to be having a good time."

"She's from a large family too, so we were swapping big family stories." Lucy stopped, tears forming in her eyes. "You know, they're waiting for me."

"Who's waiting for you?"

"My family. I see them in the room sometimes. Especially the mornings when I think I won't wake up. They want me to come and join them."

Since that dream I'd had about the Basile family portrait, I wondered how my mom's brothers and sisters looked when beckoned to her. But, thanks to Liz's advice, I'd stopped questioning or correcting my mom whenever she talked like this.

"She's in her own place," Liz explained one night when we were doing double duty since Lucy had stopped breathing earlier that afternoon, and we both thought tonight was going to be *the* night.

But it wasn't.

"She's at peace, so don't tell her she's not seeing what she's seeing or not hearing what she's hearing. It's all part of the process."

"Some process," I mumbled.

"It's beautiful," Liz added. "Dying is part of living, and the way little Lucy is dying is a beautiful thing."

"If you say so."

Replaying that conversation, I'd stopped paying attention to what my mother was saying.

"Sorry, mom, I missed that. What did you say?"

"Weren't you paying attention? I told you to get back to basics. With the story. Keep it here at All Saints. In my apartment even. And the Wii bowling thing is fun. Keep that in."

"Gee, thanks, Mom," I smiled, then scrunched my body and gave her a conspiratorial look. "You know that's where all the murder victims are going to come from, don't you?"

"I suspected that," she nodded. "So, hop to it. Bring me more chapters. We don't have much more time you know."

"Mom don't talk like that. Who knows how long we have?"

She gave me the usual pat on the hand that told me I was wrong. "Sweetie, I know alright. And it isn't that long."

chapter fourteen
AWOL

Over the course of the nearly six weeks since my mom had decided to die, I pretty much kept to my public speaking schedule for the UW and actually did make a handful of presentations statewide. Those appearances kept me sane, not to mention that nearly every time someone in the audience would be moved by the music and stories.

Pam and Liz, even Lucy, had encouraged me to do this, so I did. Only two of the talks were out-of-town and just one, a very special event in St. Paul, Minnesota, marking the end of their yearlong Vietnam War retrospective, required an overnight. Nevertheless, it pained me to say goodbye to my mom whenever I left her. Summoning my old Catholic guilt, I was convinced that she would die while I was away, and I'd hate myself forever for not being there when she took her last breath.

The phone conversations I had with her whenever I was at a distance didn't help much either. Disconcerting, to say the least. When I was returning from a community south of Milwaukee late one night, I called and Liz put her on. Lucy seem delighted that she was going to see me the next day, but when Liz got back on the phone, she explained to me that my mom had thought I was Ron.

"Is she doing that a lot?" I asked.

"Doing what? You mean confusing you with Ron?"

"I guess…maybe her just being more confused?"

"Doug," Liz's voice became low and soothing, "she's dying. She's getting closer. It's part of the process."

"You said that before," I fired back, hitting the accelerator harder as I drove.

"I'll admit it's taken longer with Lucy. She's a lot stronger than any of us realized. Herself included. But it's getting close. Confusion is part of it. Her breathing's changed. Her heartbeat. Her body temp is lower…"

"How soon?" I started sobbing.

"I honestly don't know," Liz admitted. "But it won't be much longer."

"Will she know who I am when I see her tomorrow?"

"If she's awake. She's sleeping almost all the time now. But I didn't correct her just now and say it was you. I just let it go. It's better that way…"

Of course, this latest development made me even more nervous about going to Minnesota. I was in effect the closing act of the PBS station's final evening, so I hated to let them down. Pam made it somewhat easier by purchasing a round-trip plane ticket so I wouldn't have to drive. I'd be gone less than 24 hours, but…

The only way I could manage the separation and not think about maybe missing my mom's death was to force myself to write more of the mystery. Which is what I did that night at the hotel after all the post-event festivities had wrapped up for the evening. Not like I was going to sleep anyway. If my mom wanted more of Father Paul, I'd give it to her.

"It was mid-morning by the time Father Paul arrived back at the Good Shepherd rectory. The usually energetic 60-something priest was exhausted. And thoroughly perplexed, too, by what had recently transpired at Old Saints. But he had to put all that on hold for the time being, since God's work always came first when he was back on sacred premises. "My landlord," Father Paul would point to the sky and smilingly tell his parishioners, "expects me to work for my rent."

In addition to the usual entreaties from his parishioners, Father Paul anxiously anticipated a slew of messages from local media about the lethal events at Old Saints. But for the moment, it seemed that his old pal Melvin had been able to keep the story—and Father Paul's name—out of the papers. "Thank God for small favors," the priest said to himself, examining the usual assortment of yellow message slips from sad widows, weary widowers, wayward souls, and prankster teens.

First order of business was for Father Paul to get his energy back, and for that he'd need a pot of the strongest coffee east of the Mississippi, courtesy of his housekeeper, Mrs. Callahan.

"Mrs. Callahan?" he spoke into the intercom. "Are you there dear?"

"Glory be to God, Father, I'm here for another day thanks be to Jesus," came the welcoming, upbeat reply. Mrs. Callahan was always cheerful, even if her own life was anything but. Her ability to overcome a myriad of personal tragedies—losing a husband and a son and a granddaughter—spoke to a reservoir of faith that even Father Seamus Paul found astounding. But there it was, in the voice and the outlook and demeanor of one Mrs. Sheila Callahan.

"What can I do for you Father?" Had she been asking him this the whole time?

"Mrs. C., can you please brew up a pot of your most potent potable and deliver it to me ASAP!"

"I'm way ahead of you Father," said the familiar friendly voice. "Coffee is ready. I'll bring it up as soon as my blueberry muffins are out of the oven."

"God bless you Mrs. Callahan," the priest responded with unexpected enthusiasm.

"Don't mention it Father. I'll be straight up." She paused. "Oh, and Father, Bishop Florentino called …"

Father Paul's heart sank. Nothing good could come of a conversation with Bishop Florentino, the local diocese's ecclesiastic leader who seemed to have it in for Father Paul ever since he'd arrived from upstate New York. Florentino was much too conservative for this conclave of feisty, independent Roman Catholics, and Father Paul often found himself in the middle of the diocesan disagreements. It didn't help either that Florentino knew of

Seamus Paul's previous career, prompting him to call him "chief" even in public.

Father Paul knew he'd be gone from Madison if it weren't for the intercession of his mentor, Monsignor Michael Mayweather, who navigated the slippery terrain between Father Paul and the prickly bishop. Mayweather understood better than most the politics of the church, and the community, and he was somehow able to keep the diocese and its leaders out of trouble.

He even said Mass at Old Saints twice a week and visited the dying residents. The Monsignor always gave Father Paul the strength to carry on and advise him how to deal with the wrath of Bishop Dominic Florentino.

Mrs. Callahan's smiling face appeared in the doorway, a tray of steaming hot coffee, his favorite Green Bay Packers mug, cream and sugar, and a plate of blueberry muffins adorning the tray she was carrying. For a moment, Father Paul felt like he was taking communion.

"Did the Bishop's office leave a message?" he asked Mrs. Callahan as she put down the tray.

"That media liaison or spoked person or whatever he is..."

"Will Murphy," Father Paul interrupted.

"Yes, that's him," Mrs. Callahan nodded. "I don't know why a bishop needs a personal messenger, do you father? I thought we all spoke with one voice, God's voice?" She seemed genuinely perplexed.

"Yes, well, it's the times we live in Mrs. C.. What did Mr. Murphy say the Bishop wanted anyway?"

"He asked where you were and said to call him as soon as you were back." She paused, looking worriedly at the man she adored like a son. "Is everything alright Father?"

"Lord yes," a distracted Father Paul replied. "Thank you, Mrs. C.. God bless."

Mrs. Callahan took that as her cue to leave. Father Paul slowly punched in the Bishop's direct line, which he knew would be answered by Will Murphy, yet another of his nemeses. Small towns will do that, *thought Father Paul, remembering Murphy as a beat reporter with the local paper back when he was chief of police. Murphy was the kind of person who never trusted anyone, always suspected someone of something. That distrust played out in his coverage of the police department when Father Paul was in charge. More often than not, then Chief of Police Seamus Paul's press briefings ended with a disgruntled Murphy waving from the back of the room, complaining he didn't get called on.*

Father Paul's primary problem with Will Murphy was that when he didn't have the answers, he'd make them up. That eventually got Murphy in trouble with his paper, but then his career was surprisingly resurrected by Bishop Florentino who named him the diocese's first ever spokesperson. In his new role, Murphy brought along the same disdain he had for Seamus Paul as chief of police, prompting Father Paul to view Will Murphy as his personal "cross to bear."

But it was a cross he'd just as soon not have to carry today.

"Bishop Florentino's office. Will Murphy speaking," said the curt voice on the other end of the line. "Blessings to you and yours."

"Will, this is Father Paul."

"Father Flatfoot, where the hell have you been?" came the accusatory tone. Father Paul winced.

"Conducting the lord's work, as I do every day," the priest responded politely.

"I hope for your sake you weren't at Old Saints last night," Murphy bullied him, "because I've been on the phone with several very affluent Old Saints residents who said there was a suspicious death there last night. One of them claimed she saw you there."

Silence at the other end of the line.

"Well, were you?" Murphy insisted.

"Was I what?"

"Were you at Old Saints last night?"

"Briefly," Father Paul responded.

"How briefly?"

"I was asked to give the Last Rites to one of the residents but I arrived too late," admitted Father Paul. "Mrs. Bessie Procter had already gone to meet her maker."

"May she rest in peace," Murphy replied mechanically. Father Paul thought he could hear Murphy doing the math in his head if, by divine intervention, the wealthy Mrs. Procter would bequeath any of her abundance to the diocese.

"Anyway, get your cassock and collar over here, the Bishop wants to see you."

"Is it about Ms. Procter?"

"What? No," Murphy replied distractedly. "I was just trying to put the other two and two together."

"Then what does the Bishop want to see me about?"

"Bad news," Murphy shot back. "Monsignor Mayweather died."

I looked back over what I'd written. Not bad. Not quite sure where the Monsignor's death came from; in fact, it sort of wrote itself. I'd tie that in with the other Old Saints deaths too—I was leaving enough cookie crumbs for readers to follow and smiled gleefully because Will Murphy and Bishop Florentino would be the masterminds behind all the Old Saints murders, including Monsignor Mayweather's. Now that will piss off a lot of Catholics, but they had it coming. But why did I use Monsignor Mayweather's real name? I made a note to myself to change it lest Lucy give me a hard time for using real names. Again.

I'd left my car at the airport so I could zip right over to my mom's when I landed. I couldn't wait to read her the latest. She'd love finding out more about Father Paul. And since I knew now where the story was heading, it would be smooth sailing. I could finish this puppy in no time!

As my plane touched down, I imagined the cover of our book—a photo of the All Saints Retirement Center shrouded in ominous clouds, the title, *Saints and Sinners,* in big letters superimposed on the dark clouds, the names of the two authors at the bottom, "A Father Paul mystery by Lucy Bradley & Son."

Wouldn't a potential book tour be reason enough for my mom to stay alive?

chapter fifteen

Time to Go

"Some people die like they live," a hospice social worker appropriately named Grace explained to me as we sat in the living room of my mom's apartment. We'd just begun week seven of Lucy's oh so slow march toward death, so maybe Grace and hospice figured we were nearing the end?

"I'm guessing your mother lived life fully, strongly…busily," she added. I smiled at that adjective, recalling how my mother indeed was in constant motion, always "busy" doing something. Even now. Busily trying to die.

Grace looked like a Grace—grey hair in a neat bun, slight frame, long brown dress, a burnt orange scarf around her neck. Older woman's shoes, too. Unlike her name, Grace didn't bestow all that many blessings. None upon Lucy at least, checking up more on my mental state, judging from her questions. When she finished talking, she handed me a large folder, chock full of snazzy looking materials with handy tips for grieving and surviving. A list of hospice support groups I could join, too. All accompanied by multiple donation forms if I chose to contribute to the local hospice for all their help and support.

I did appreciate what the hospice folks were doing, even if I had to spend too much time keeping them, Liz's crew, and CARE Wisconsin on the same page. And with no idea how long this would go on, all we could do was keep our faith, and trust in Liz since she'd spent the most time with all of us and had a much better feel for where things were with Lucy. I guess that qualified her as a death doula alright.

I got a real appreciation for Liz's special skills the day I came back from Minnesota. I was eager to read my mom the new *Saints and Sinners* piece I'd worked on while I was away, but all Lucy wanted to do was get out of bed. And quick.

"Mom, lie still so I can read this new part to you. I think you're gonna like it."

"I don't have time for stories," she replied breathlessly. "They're waiting for me. I have to go."

"Go where, Mom? And with who?"

"My family. They're all waiting for me. Help me get dressed." She started to pull at her turquoise nightgown.

"Mom, you're not going anywhere. And don't take your clothes off."

"You don't understand." She sounded dejected. "I have to get dressed and go. They're waiting. It's time."

This went on for almost 15 minutes before Liz came in with ice chips, flowers, and a big smile. Unlike Grace, Liz was dressed like spring, a bright, multi-colored, flowing dress, a necklace, and smart-looking sandals.

"How's little Lucy?"

"Not good." My mom was still struggling with her nightie. I hadn't seen this much energy from her in weeks. "Doug won't let me go."

Liz gave me a sympathetic look, then titled her head toward the door for me to take my leave. Frustrated as usual by the situation, I sat in the kitchen, fussing and writing in my journal. After a while I could hear laughter coming from the bedroom. Lots and lots of laughter. After a few more minutes, Liz emerged.

"What's going on?" I asked, perturbed.

"She's asleep," came Liz's reply.

"What was all that about anyway?"

"Your mother's dying, Doug," Liz's voice was decisive, yet soothing. When she placed her hand on mine, I burst into tears.

"I know she is and I'm sorry. I'm just trying to help."

"I know you are. More importantly, Lucy knows you are. But sometimes we lose patience. Especially when a loved one is getting close to passing."

"So when is this happening?" My daily $64,000 question.

Liz smiled. "Soon."

"How do you know?"

"You see the color of her skin? It's nearly grey. I told you about the breathing and body temperature and the rest. And the weakness."

"She seems strong to me."

"Mentally, yes. Determined. Determined to die. But she has no muscles, no body strength. That's what we were laughing about."

"Come again?"

"When she told me she wanted to get dressed and go, unlike you, I told her to go ahead, to get up and get dressed. And guess what happened?"

"I'm past playing guessing games."

"She couldn't get herself out of bed," Liz laughed. "Every time she tried to get upright or move her legs and put them on the side of the bed, she collapsed back, laughing. She was too weak to get out of bed."

"So is this some kind of reverse psychology I need to try out?"

"No, it's just understanding where a dying person is at. Like I told you before, don't waste your time telling her she can't get dressed or that there isn't anybody waiting for her. Just let it go. Let *her* go. Let her die the way she wants."

Maybe it was my worry about taking the trip. Or my guilt about having left town in the first place? Whatever, I was an emotional wreck and just sat in my mother's tiny kitchen and cried like a baby as Liz rubbed my back and whispered that I was doing a good job and that everything was going to be okay.

chapter sixteen

"My Ideal"

Liz was right about letting my mom go where she wanted to go, although there was less and less of that day by day. She'd likewise nailed Lucy's prognosis judging by my mom's nearly constant sleeping, erratic breathing, sallow look, and occasional unconsciousness. Days 42, 43, 44, and 45 fused into one continuous 96-hour groundhog day interrupted briefly by fits of frenzied behavior when Lucy tried to get out of bed or pointed out that there was someone else, or several someones, besides us, who was there in her bedroom. Ghosts only she could see. Pam and I were tag teaming the around-the-clock coverage with Liz's team and hospice. All the elderly care, near-death experts agreed Lucy's end was near, but for those of us on duty, it was another day in my mom's wanting-to-die marathon.

Alone with my mom in her bedroom, watching her waste away moment by moment, I thought about giving her the morphine that now sat nearby on her nightstand…or gently placing one of the pillows over her face. Despicable temptations, yes, but I so desperately wanted her to finally have some peace.

But I would never forgive myself if I did anything as horrible as that.

Instead I read aloud the latest *Saints and Sinners* segment about Father Paul. And then I recited everything I'd written as if Lucy was still listening, still editing…maybe even approving?

But there was no visible response from my once persnickety editor. How I missed those repeated Lucy interruptions. For sure she would've weighed in on the Father Paul-Bishop Florentino dynamic. Would ask me why Monsignor Mayweather had to die…Now that I thought about that, I couldn't remember if it was the Monsignor or some other All Saints priest who had stopped by to give her the last rites…

I also dealt several hands of her favorite card game, pinochle, the two-handed version we used to play, seated at her kitchen table beneath the kitchen light with blue sailboats on the lampshade and the tiny pull-string chain. And, like always, the hands I dealt to her were the winning ones. Inky, wherever he was, would nod in agreement.

At the advice of the caregivers, I called Ron and put the phone next to my mom's ear so he could say goodbye. I couldn't hear what he was saying, but my mom's eyes opened and her mouth moved a little, but nothing came out. Was she in that moment recalling every moment of their 75 years together? She and Ron had so much in common—they read mysteries voraciously, knocked out the daily crossword puzzle and jumble like champions, and had some unspoken connection. Maybe it was the few years they spent together, just the two of them, while our dad was overseas during World War II? Or maybe it was the nights they'd stay up late and watch old movies on TV and laugh their fool heads off at something hilarious Cary Grant or Mr. Hulot had done? Whatever it was, it was something, something binding and unexplainable. But I heard it in the crackling of the cellphone as they said their last goodbye.

All four of Ron and Carol's children had been able to get to Wisconsin and say goodbye to their last remaining grandma, so no need for those phone calls. Plus, I could tell the call to Ron had taken something out of Lucy. But Summer and Ian had spent lots of time with my folks after Pam and I moved them here in 2006, so I placed calls to both of them. Summer's more stoic than most, but I could hear her sniffling and saying, "I love you grandma," a sentiment that had taken on added currency now that Summer herself was a mom.

Ian seemed to get to her. I noticed a lot more eye and mouth movement during his call, testament to their special bond. And maybe some residual sadness at the wedding she'd missed.

But Lucy's biggest, most animated response was to music. I played her an old ballad called "My Ideal," the Bing Crosby version from YouTube, and you would have thought Der Bingle himself was in the room. At the song's opening line, "Will I ever find the girl in my mind," Lucy's face lit up, momentarily the wrinkles and the grey skin color were gone, and she honest-to-goodness smiled. So I played the song again, and she had the same life-altering reaction. It was a minor miracle.

From the books I've written and the presentations I've given about the music-based memories of Vietnam veterans, I know about the science behind the powerful connection between music and memory. Sounds, songs, strike the hippocampus in the exact spot where memory lives. But it wasn't until I googled the lyrics and followed along as I replayed "My Ideal," that I realized it was a song my father used to sing to my mom. In fact, it was *their* song. Had I known this all along? Or was my dad here now in the bedroom with us, his melodious voice crooning, "Maybe she's a dream, and yet she might be/Just around the corner waiting for me."

I played that song multiple times for my mom, crying as I listened, picturing my mom in my father's arms as he serenaded her as his "ideal." Which she was for Jack Bradley. And now my dad…he was patiently waiting for her too. In the room now maybe?

★★★

Day 49 of Lucy's "hunger strike" augured more of the same. A Saturday at the end of June, so there wouldn't be any hospice nurses. I took the early, early morning shift. Pam brought me lunch which we ate at Lucy's bedside. Little progress or regress. When Liz arrived later that afternoon, she and Pam convinced me to go home and try to get some sleep. The cell phone by my side, I dozed fitfully, hearing my dad singing "My Ideal" in the next room. Seeing my mom as a younger, happier, healthier version of herself. The two of them so deeply in love. A model marriage, another gift to me and my brother.

Then I saw the light of the phone before I heard it ringing.

"Doug, it's happening," came Liz's breathless voice. "Come quick."

chapter seventeen

The Long Goodbye

I'm not a total skeptic by nature, but I pooh pooed those fairy tale stories about how the death of a loved one can be beautiful or whatever. The agony of my father's final moments—a loud, discomforting, gurgling death rattle that went on for hours—convinced me that such occasions were less than dreamy. And now my mother? Strange that both my Philadelphia-bred parents would die in Madison, Wisconsin, my dad's early training station during World War II. The place where my mother refused to move because he told her the lakes froze, the city where my wife-to-be would grow up and go to college. Where I would get married, raise a family, live and work for going on 50 years…

Was that all predetermined when Jack Bradley was a lowly Army private at Truax Field in 1943? Did some part of him remain here that called to me and brought me here? For not having lofty thoughts about dying, I sure was being awfully mystical about life as I drove the few miles to All Saints apartment 159.

Maybe for the last time?

Pam and Liz were in the bedroom, tears in their eyes. Pam sat at the foot of my mom's bed, Liz seated on the right in that run-down desk chair my mom used when she was at her sewing machine. Lucy's sewing, mending, and tailoring days were over. How many hats and scarves and mittens and clothes had she made for me and my family over the years? Had we ever properly thanked her? Ever?

I sat in the hardbacked chair next to my mom and pulled up as close as I could, grasping her withered left hand in mine, pressing it tight, as if asking it if anyone was home. Liz had washed and dressed Lucy in the bright turquoise nightgown and put a bright blue garland around her neck. She looked more than peaceful. Almost happy. And ready to go somewhere…

We watched her chest move up and down, slowly. Sometimes not moving at all. She was completely still, waiting. None of us spoke. I kept sending Morse code messages through her hand, gently tapping *I'm here; I love you. I'll miss you…you are the best mom,* until I broke down.

Then started doing it all over again…

I'm not sure how long we kept vigil. Time had stopped in a way, and we were with Lucy on her journey. Time didn't matter. There was only this *now*. And then my mom's whole body seemed to lift, starting with her head which pulled forward and upward off the pillow, her eyes, closed, but pointing toward the ceiling. And then her shoulders arched and rose aloft, making her body ascend somehow. It was as if she had wings. Holding her hand I could feel it. She'd lifted, risen, and left.

Lucy Bradley was gone. Back home, finally, with that loud, sprawling Italian family she loved so much. To dancing in the dark in my father's arms as he sang "My Ideal," to all the comforts she gave me and Ron, to knitting and sewing and crossword puzzles and card playing. And winning. Lucy was a winner alright. Even though it took her seven weeks, 49 days, she went out on her own terms, went up, up, and away in the process.

Time returned, and with it we last three of Lucy's supplicants. We dried our eyes, blew our noses, hugged a little. Then we picked up my mom's room, still with her in it. I called the Dane County Coroner's office and tried not to break down.

But now I wanted to be alone with my mother. Just the two of us. So I encouraged Pam and Liz to leave and I'd handle the coroner and all the rest. That gave me time to have a last word with my mom, but I couldn't stop crying.

Finally, just as there was a knock on the door, I collected myself and looked down in Lucy's eyes.

"Once upon a time," I began with a whisper…

chapter eighteen

The Rest of the Story

If this were a Hollywood movie or TV show, *Saints and Sinners* would end up being published and become a best seller. Maybe adapted as a movie? The Father Paul mystery series would propel me into the national spotlight. Lucy would have legions of fans everywhere, begging her to come back and write a sequel…blah blah blah.

But it's not a movie. It isn't fiction. My mother of 99 years decided after she turned 99 that she didn't want to live anymore and elected to die. And it took her 49 long days to do it. End of story.

Well, not quite.

While Ron had done a terrific job of cleaning out my mom's apartment while he was here, he hadn't gotten rid of everything. At that point, Lucy was still alive, and she and we needed clothes and towels and sheets and all the rest. Meaning her old oak dresser had remained intact. Clearing out that dresser, selling off or donating all her stuff, and cleaning the apartment were my last orders of business. "My wholly orders," I'd joke to myself, mimicking Monsignor Mayweather's clerical tone.

The whole business struck me as odd, and sad—is this all that's left of a person's life, one that nearly spanned a century? Clothes, sheets, and pillowcases; yarn and fabric. Wasn't my mom more than this? More than all of it put together? "More precious was the light in your eyes than all the roses in the world," I repeated those lines of a poem I knew by Edna St. Vincent Millay. That was Lucy and her light. Better than any rose. Or the things she'd left behind.

Turns out the old oak dresser had a few surprises in store, three items that would have made a genuine mystery aficionado like my mom salivate. And shed a little more light on just who Lucia Jean Basile Bradley was.

The first was a small, pearl handled pistol. I'd never seen it before, had no idea it even existed. Did it belong to my mom's immigrant father Giuseppe? Or any of her six older Albanian-Italian brothers? Given their roots, maybe the pistol helped keep the Mafia away? After a little research, we realized it was a starter pistol, not a real one. But that made it even more of a mystery. Why did my mother have it? Where did she get it? Did she ever use it? Just what was she *starting* anyway? Questions that would never be answered.

The second discovery was a pair of yellowed letters, rubber-banded together, that had been mailed to my father's mother, Lucy's mother-in-law, who also was named Lucia. Lucia Shumway, later Bradley, lived a life totally antithetical to my mom's. Lonely and sad, Lucia Shumway married an abusive, philandering husband who left her poor and heartbroken, smothering my dad, her only child, in the process. No wonder Jack Bradley so loved the noise and chaos of the large Basile household,…but why would my mom keep those two letters of her mother-in-law, Lucia Bradley? One, dated 1930, was a long, detailed, descriptive horoscope from some paranormal wackos in New York City that must have cost my grandmother a lot of money. Whatever they were purporting, none of it seemed to change her life any.

The second letter, postmarked Kansas City, Missouri, 1939, was from the Unity School of Christianity, encouraging Lucia Bradley to take heart and to pray and pray and pray if she wanted her son (my father) to find gainful employment. And, by the way, when you're not praying, send the Unity School of Christianity some money if you please! My dad was 19 when his mother received the letter, and while I'm not sure what job it was that he was pursuing at the time, I do know that he and his mother were gone from his father by then, although they were almost penniless. My dad desperately needed to get a good-paying job in order for the two of them to survive. But did he get <u>that</u> job? And did his mother's prayers, and payments, to the Unity School of Christianity, make a difference? Did my mom still have those because my father had kept them and she couldn't bear to throw them away, erase any memories of his? Or because she and his mother shared the same first name? Too many questions into the stale apartment air than would ever be answered…

The last surprise was a book of my mom's old recipes. The card taped on the inside front cover said it was the property of "Toots" Basil (sic), 1245 S. 47th Street. Lucy's old family nickname was "Toots" because she loved to eat Tootsie Rolls. The ink in the recipe book had faded, and it was hard to make out the details on the pages upon pages of family recipes. I've learned some of these over the years, including her world class spaghetti and meatballs. Even more interesting were the interlinear pages between recipes when it appeared my mom was writing down lyrics from songs or else swooning about musicians and bandleaders she had a crush on. I couldn't make it out very well, but she'd written a lot about one particular big band leader named *Skinnay Ennis* with a lot of xxx's and ooo's by his name. The more I said the name aloud, the more I realized it was *his* name she was calling out that day in her sleep— "Skinnay Ennis" and <u>not</u> "Dennis the Menace." Hard to picture any other man in my mom's life other than Jack Bradley, but I guess I could've been Skinnay Jr. if her wildest dreams had come true.

I gave almost everything away, including the starter pistol, only keeping the two letters and the recipe book. They keep Lucy's ashes company in the space they occupy above my desk. I put the pages of *Saints and Sinners* in there too just in case she might like to read them over again some time. I don't see how I could ever finish that mystery without her around to critique and improve it…to critique and improve me.

In the end I realized the story my mom wanted me to read to her, the one she wanted me to write, was this one. I sure hope she's listening.

Acknowledgements

There's probably some rule about not acknowledging the same person you dedicate the book to. Maybe it's a bigger sin if that person is also the subject of your story? Guilty on both counts as I acknowledge my mother, Lucy Jean Basile Bradley, for all she did and all she was for me and my family.

And acclaim to my family, too, all of whom I so deeply love, for their affection for Lucy—my spouse Pam Shannon, my children Summer and Ian, their spouses Brandon and Mary; my brother and best friend Ron, spouse Carol, and their children Michael, Nicole, Tim, and Kevin, and their spouses Jessica and Skylar. And all Lucy's great grandchildren—Bella, Oliver, Penelope, Emma, Noah, Alexander, Tess, Bowie, Lucia, and Teddy.

Thanks, too, for all the support our friends gave us and my mom, in particular Lucy's "adopted" son Don Mash and partner Sharon Ehrmeyer.

And a very special thanks to Lucy's pilot, attendant, and guide on her final journey, Liz Humphries. She and her Seasons of Life colleagues kept Lucy in her home, and in their hearts, during her last weeks and days.

There are helpful resources such as Death With Dignity (https:// deathwithdignity.org) if/when your loved one wants to consider alternatives. My advice is to be patient, don't go it alone, and hold on to their hand as long as you can.

Doug Bradley, Fall 2025

About the Author

Doug Bradley is an author, educator, and Vietnam veteran whose work often explores the intersections of memory, culture, war, and family. He has written four books, most recently *The Tracks of My Years*, a music-based memoir, and has contributed to PBS's *Next Avenue* and *The Huffington Post*. He taught for many years at the University of Wisconsin–Madison, Baldwin Wallace University, and Arizona State University.

Three of his earlier books are rooted in the Vietnam experience, including *DEROS Vietnam: Dispatches from the Air-Conditioned Jungle, Who'll Stop the Rain: Respect, Remembrance, and Reconciliation in Post-Vietnam America,* and *We Gotta Get Out of This Place: The Soundtrack of the Vietnam War*, named Best Music Book of 2015 by *Rolling Stone.*

"With a veteran's wisdom, a father's heart, and a storyteller's gift, Doug Bradley reminds us that our memories don't just mark our past—they shape who we become and help us find our way forward." ~ Erin Celello, author, *Learning to Stay*